About the Author

Dogged by illness and a myriad debilitating ailments in her early twenties, Mary-Ann Shearer began her personal quest for a common-sense approach to health and vitality. This led to what was to become a life-long interest in studying and researching natural health, and culminated in her development of the Natural Way dietary programme.

This simple yet effective lifestyle plan has produced astonishing results for thousands of people who have learned to understand and correct their diet-related problems.

In her efforts to show just how easy it is to be healthy, Mary-Ann wrote *The Natural Way: A Family's Guide to Vibrant Health,* a book which has become the best-selling title on health in Southern Africa. She has also compiled a selection of tried and tested recipes in *The Natural Way Recipe Book 1* and *The Natural Way Recipe Book 2*, and is currently working on several new titles, the first of which (*Good Food, Healthy Kids*) will be published in November 2000.

For more information on the Natural Way programme, log on to Mary-Ann's website at *www.mary-anns.com* or call her info line on 083 910 1548, 24 hours a day at normal cellular phone rates. The info line provides answers to the most commonly-asked questions, new recipes and health tips, and updated information on Mary-Ann's products, talks, cookery demonstrations and support groups.

THE
NATURAL WAY

A FAMILY'S GUIDE TO VIBRANT HEALTH

Mary-Ann Shearer

Ibis Books
Cape Town

ISBN 0 9583927 2 2

This edition published in 1995 by
Ibis Books and Editorial Services cc
P O Box 136 Muizenberg 7950
reprinted in 1996 (twice), 1997, 1999,
2000 (twice) and 2001.

Set in 11.8 on 13 pt Times
Design and phototypesetting by Book Productions, Pretoria
Printed and bound by Clyson Printers, Cape Town

Acknowledgements

Without the support and love of my husband Mark, this book would never have been written, and without the wisdom from God I would still be battling with my so-called allergies.

My deep gratitude must go to my family – Mark and my three daughters, Melissa, Marie-Claire and Meredith – for allowing me to 'experiment' on them.Their glowing health and well-being has been a rich reward.

To my mother, Angelique Van Hoogstraten, thank you for instilling in me that seed of health consciousness.

To all the people I have been able to help over the past years, I am indebted to you for allowing me to use your case studies.

To all those many people who have helped me to challenge and research what I believed was true, thank you – this book is for all of you.

This book does not presume to be a prescription. Rather, it is intended to help you understand your body and to assist you in making healthier decisions about your diet and lifestyle.

Contents

Foreword

Since first putting pen to paper in 1989, a lot more research has been done in the field of nutrition and its relationship to health. All of it has backed up and confirmed the basic principles in *The Natural Way*, with many researchers being quite outspoken about the fact that if we don't eat more fruit and vegetables (suggestions range from 5 – 11 portions daily), we won't be able to avoid the Big Three, namely heart disease, diabetes and cancer. So although times, places and dates have been updated in this edition, nothing else has changed concerning the Natural Way programme, other than adding a much-needed index.

During the four years that *The Natural Way* has been on the shelves, I have received hundreds of letters from all over the world from people whose health has improved dramatically just by changing their eating habits. Sinusitis, asthma, diabetes, ME, lupus, digestive disorders, cancer and even Aids have been some of the symptoms that they have recovered from.These letters just serve to confirm that when we treat our bodies the way they were designed to be treated, they will respond with vital glowing health, and although the return to health might take a good few months, the effort is always worth it!

This is a testimony to a world-wide phenomenon of growing health consciousness. Health and healthy living are no longer reserved for the 'weirdos' or 'cranks' but have become mainstream. It is now even fashionable to be health-conscious. In fact, you cannot afford not to take responsibility for your own health.

To those of you battling to maintain a healthier life-style, keep looking back to see how far you have come, don't set unrealistic goals or standards for yourself or for your family, and remember that you cannot change your life-style overnight. It has taken 20, 30, 40 or even 80 years to get your body into a certain state, and you cannot expect to undo the damage in two days or even two weeks. The Natural Way is a slow, step-by-step lifetime commitment to a healthier, more energetic and happier you.

To Health! May God bless and keep you from day to day.

Mary-Ann
June 1995

CHAPTER ONE

The Shearer Family: How Our Diet and Health Evolved

Why have I written this book? The reasons are many.

Ever since I first became interested in nutrition in my late teens, I have wanted to discover the secret of being in charge of my own health. Perhaps this sounds pretentious, but when I looked at animals in the wild and compared them with domesticated animals, I began to realise that diet and lifestyle play a major role in attaining health and well-being. Have you ever seen or heard of an overweight springbuck suffering from gout, ear infections or osteoporosis? Neither have I! Have you ever encountered a domesticated cat or dog suffering from these ailments? Me too!

In my search, I read just about any health book and article I could lay my hands on. The result? Total confusion! And what's more, I was branded the 'health nut'!

There I was, drinking apple cider vinegar and honey to start my day, followed by my own home-made muesli with my own home-made yoghurt and unheated natural honey. I would drink mostly herbal teas, an occasional cup of Ceylon tea and, very rarely, a cup of decaffeinated coffee. This was followed by lunch, usually my own home-made bread with light margarine, even lighter cottage cheese, and a still lighter health salt. Perhaps I'd have a slice of tomato or some lettuce for variety. Oh! I'd almost forgotten the vitamins I would always take after a meal. There'd be calcium, vitamin A (for skin and eyes), vitamin B (complex of course) for pre-menstrual tension, hair and nails, vitamin C for colds and flu, and many more besides. Supper would consist of vegetables with unpolished rice (naturally) and fish, chicken or red meat limited to two or three times a week only.

So what was wrong? The problem was, I was suffering from severe dermatitis on my hands and I had been sneezing non-stop for about a year. My children suffered from ear infections, tonsillitis and runny noses, all deemed to be perfectly normal by society's standards. Oh yes, the indigestion suffered by my husband and myself – antacids were always an item on my monthly shopping list. All perfectly normal?

As a child I had to cope with the 'normal' childhood diseases, and the only problem I seemed to have repeatedly was that fever blisters kept appearing with irritating regularity. (I have since discovered that whenever I eat anything containing egg, this reaction is triggered off.) The first health problem I encountered in adulthood was recurrent indigestion – this surfaced after I had been married for a couple of years. Mark, my husband, also suffered from this problem even though we ate relatively simple food. Then I started having problems with my hands. I developed severe dermatitis between my fingers and on my palms. At this stage I thought I had merely inherited my mother's problem, and followed the same route she had – to the doctor. He, after taking one look at my hands, prescribed the same cream that my mother used, which, not surprisingly, did the same as it had for her – absolutely nothing!

Then followed what I refer to as the 'guinea-pig' stage of the treatment. Various creams, including cortisone-based products, were 'applied to the affected area', but to no avail. I was then told not to let my hands ever get sweaty, as when wearing gloves. I stopped getting soap of any description onto my skin. (To this day Mark still washes the dishes!) But none of these precautions made any difference to my condition.

After about three or four years of battling along and hiding my hands from view, a third health problem manifested itself. I started sneezing. Not just an occasional sneeze, but continual sneezing accompanied by an ever-streaming nose. The only time my nose wasn't streaming, was when it was blocked. Can you imagine my frustration? After all, I was so health-conscious! In fact, I became the family joke. 'Why don't you eat junk like us, then you'll be as healthy as we are,' they taunted. Off I traipsed to the doctor – again. This time various nasal sprays were prescribed and heat treatment was provided by a physiotherapist. This cleared my nose for an hour or two. Then the symptoms came back, with a vengeance!

Perhaps you think I exaggerate, but I assure you that I do not! My problem was so severe that I couldn't sleep properly at night. And I was keeping Mark awake too. As a result of these wakeful nights, I fell pregnant with my third daughter, and I became concerned about the possible effects that all the medication I'd been taking would have on my unborn child. I then took myself off to a homeopath.

I was most impressed! She spent nearly an hour asking me about my circumstances – where I grew up, what type of background I came from, what type of marriage I had. Finally she announced that if it weren't for the fact that I was so happily married and that I was such a happy person, I'd be extremely ill. She declared my constitution to be very sensitive. I would, therefore, have to stop eating the foods of the deadly nightshade family: tomatoes, potatoes, brinjals and green peppers. I also had to swallow a series of powders. I followed all these instructions to the letter. The result? No improvement whatsoever! I was then instructed to cut out pineapples and bananas, but this still left me sneezing and scratching my hands ... and very disillusioned.

Then one Sunday while Mark was reading the paper, he

came across a book review on *Food Combining for Health*. Apparently, this was the book to get if you suffered from allergies of any description. I was a bit sceptical after all my failed experiments, and I'm sure you understand why, but Mark suggested I give it a try. What had I to lose? I was encouraged by the fact that this time there were no drugs, powders or pills; and that I could eat all the foods I had cut out from my diet under instruction from the homeopath. All I had to ensure was that I did not eat complex carbohydrates with concentrated protein (refer to the chart at the back of the book and to the chapter on food combining). Although it sounded rather strange, the reasoning made sense.

The results were unbelievable: I stopped sneezing immediately, and four days later my hands were totally clear. But ever sceptical, I thought, 'Let's see how long this lasts'.

Mark and I no longer suffered from indigestion, and two weeks later my many symptoms had not returned. After two months I thought I was totally cured and returned to my old way of eating. The first morning after I had eaten a 'normal' supper, I woke up with a streaming nose and noticed the little tell-tale blisters between my fingers. This had to be coincidence I told myself. Anyway, how could I live without lasagne for the rest of my life? Needless to say, the indigestion returned, and the dermatitis flourished and the sneezing continued. The solution was unavoidable. I had to change my life-style and my whole way of eating. Mark was supportive and agreed to change with me, and so the whole family changed too. Not only was I now completely well, but I had considerably more energy.

By this stage our friends and family had written us off as complete health freaks, and when Melissa got tonsillitis and Marie-Claire's nose streamed, they laughed, 'We thought food combining was the answer to all ills!'

What had gone wrong? How was it possible that we found ourselves outside an emergency chemist at 2.00 a.m.

one morning pouring bright red decongestant down my six-month-old baby daughter's throat? She was a breast-fed baby! How could her nose be so blocked that she could not feed from me? Was food combining truly the answer?

I went back to the books and after intensive research, I became convinced that dairy products were the culprit. I decided to persist with food combining and to see what would happen if we eliminated all dairy products from our diet. This time the change was even more dramatic. Suddenly everyone in the house began to breathe properly. Melissa, who had always slept with an open mouth (problems with her adenoids, I was told), could breathe with her mouth closed, and Meredith, who had suffered from ear infections as well as a blocked nose, could now inhale nasally with great gusto. We were all free from the respiratory complaints which we had accepted as part of our lives. I have tested the family on numerous occasions since. For two or three days I introduce a small bit of cheese, milk or even yoghurt, and this results in mucus related problems immediately – ear infections, tonsillitis, post nasal drips, runny noses, blocked noses. And the best way to clear all of this up is definitely not with antibiotics, but through a high fruit diet and plenty of fresh vegetables. Absolutely no dairy products.

I have learned an important lesson during the past years of health experimentation and research: the body heals itself if you let it.

My family have not had any health problems for years now! No ear infections. No tonsillitis. No allergies. No indigestion. No health problems of any description! In fact, we make no medical claims on our tax return. Imagine – no antibiotics, no decongestants, no antacids, no headache tablets, no nasal sprays, in fact no medication at all since we changed the way we ate.

How did we do it? More health foods, more vitamins? No! By changing our life-style, by spending less time in the kitchen and more time with one another.

I must add here that I definitely do not know everything there is to know about the human body and nutrition, and I've yet to encounter anyone else who does. I only know that I'll spend the rest of my life studying this fascinating subject, and if in the process I can help anyone who has suffered the irritating 'symptoms' of normal modern life, then I will feel that I have achieved something worthwhile.

In the following chapters I've included practical information on how to get started on the road to complete health the Natural Way and I have included research information available both locally and abroad. Don't allow yourself to become discouraged on this road to natural health, keep looking back to see how far you've come, and you'll be motivated to keep going.

Good luck!

CHAPTER TWO

Introduction to a Healthy and Uncomplicated Way of Life: The Natural Way

This book is based on the Natural Hygiene principles, which, quite simply, encourage a way of life in which the body is treated correctly. In other words, sound, uncomplicated living habits including sufficient rest, sunshine, exercise and correct nutrition are emphasised. This way of life in turn results in physical, mental and emotional well-being.

These principles go back to the creation of man. To quote Genesis 1:29, 'Then God said, "I give you every seed-bearing plant on the face of the whole earth and every tree that has fruit with seed in it. They will be yours for food." '

During the time of Hippocrates (460-377 BC), these principles were being applied. Known as the father of modern medicine, Hippocrates regarded the human body as a whole organism and he treated his patients in what we would call a 'holistic' manner, with proper diet, fresh air, and attention to life-style habits and living conditions.

Then we can look to people like Florence Nightingale, who insisted on fresh air, sunshine, wholesome food and spotlessly clean accommodation for her patients, at a time when these notions of hygiene were not widespread.

Men like Dr William Hay, Dr Herbert Shelton, Dr Henry Beiler and Dr Robert S Mendelsohn are all contemporary medical doctors who became disillusioned with what modern medicine had to offer. They realised that there is no sense in treating the symptom without first seeking out the cause. In most instances, the cause was found to be incorrect eating and poor life-style habits. These men did extensive work and documented their findings in numerous books. In 1935 Dr William Hay's *A New Health Era* was published. Dr Hay was a medical practitioner who lost faith in the abilities of medicine when he became ill and was diagnosed as being incurable. He was spurred on to research and study how life-style and diet affect health. To quote from the conclusion of his book, 'To live right, so as to cost us nothing in dissipated vitality, is easier than to live wrong'. In 1965 Dr Beiler, a medical practitioner from Capistrano Beach, recorded the findings of his research into how diet affects health in his book *Food is Your Best Medicine*. Similarly, Dr Mendelsohn published his findings in the 1980s in *Confessions of a Medical Heretic*. Dr Shelton, another medical man who practised from the 1930s to the 1980s, is the author of many books on the subject of health, life-style and diet, and he did much to capture the principles of natural hygiene in his writings. His books include: *Superior Nutrition; Health For Millions; Living Life to Live it Longer; Exercise; Food Combining Made Easy* and *The Hygienic Care of Children*, all invaluable sources of information.

The interesting thing about these men and their research is that their work and findings were totally independent of one another, and yet they seemed to reach much the same conclusion. Namely, that the body is supremely intelligent and if treated correctly and fed simply, it will always heal itself. They also discovered that by living correctly the quality of life, and death, is greatly improved.

I will attempt to show you in the following chapters how uncomplicated and sensible this way of life is.

THE INTELLIGENCE OF THE BODY

I do not intend to go into a full description of how every part of the body works. I'll be satisfied if you simply begin to understand how incredibly intelligent and wise the human body is, and how by respecting that intelligence, the quality of life improves.

Take something as simple as thirst. When your cells (everything ultimately happens at cellular level) have not received enough water with the last intake of food, or if the intake contained too much salt or other condiments (your body needs more water to dilute the toxic effect that the condiments or salt would have on the cells), they set about obtaining the water that they need to function. The cells send a message to the brain, the brain interprets the message and your throat becomes dry. You then realise that you are thirsty and you drink something. The cells have obtained their water and can go about their business once more. Now all that took place without your being aware of it!

Then, of course, there is that miracle of conception and growth in the uterus. What tells the fertilized egg to divide and multiply? What tells it to develop some cells that will form a heart and others that will form the lungs? What tells it to form certain organs of the body before others? It can only be the innate intelligence of the body. Yet we treat our bodies badly, we become ill and then expect something as inanimate as an antibiotic to have more 'intelligence' than this wondrous and complex organism.

Think of the sun, for example. Our bodies need about twenty minutes of sunshine a day. But what do we do? We lie in the sun and after about twenty minutes of sunshine we begin to feel hot and uncomfortable. Do we get out of the sun? No! We jump into the sea or a swimming-pool to cool down so that we can force our bodies to take more sunshine than they need. The result? Burning, sunstroke and even skin

11

cancer! We then say that the sun is dangerous and go to great lengths to stay out of it. We thus constantly demonstrate our lack of respect for the body's intelligence.

I will say this now and I will repeat it many times in these pages – learn to listen to your body. It is supremely intelligent!

As new-born babies we know instinctively how to listen to our bodies, and even as young children we are still aware of its messages. But as we grow older, we forget how to listen, and eventually become 'deaf'. A small child or baby will not want to eat when he is not well. The body is trying to focus all it's energy on correcting the problem at hand and does not want any food in the stomach, as digestion requires a great deal of energy. The body, in the meantime, always makes sure that it stores reserves for times like these. So what do we 'clever' adults do? 'The child won't eat,' we say. 'The child will die if he doesn't eat.' So we proceed to tempt the child with all kinds of 'treats', non-foods that in the long run pervert the child's taste-buds and do more damage than if he had not eaten at all. Remember being fed jelly and ice-cream when you weren't well as a child? Remember being coaxed to eat so that you could get well sooner? Well, you didn't get well sooner. All that happened was that you were taught not to listen to your body.

I am not trying to blame our parents for all our bad eating habits, but merely trying to show how we learned not to listen to our bodies.

WHY WE BECOME SICK AND OVERWEIGHT

Recent research completed in 1990 by Cornell University, together with help from Oxford University and various Chinese researchers, shows that diet plays a tremendous role in disease and obesity. This, the largest and most comprehensive nutritional study conducted to date, involved the diet of 6 500 Chinese people. The researchers found that these people have a high plant content in their diet as opposed to the refined, highly processed and additive-laden diet typical of many Western countries. The study shows that the diet of the Chinese promotes health, whereas that of the typical Westerner promotes disease.

Although an article appeared way back in the 6 July 1963 issue of *The Lancet*, a highly reputable medical journal, showing that people in North-west Pakistan consume the simplest possible diet of wheat, corn, potatoes and fruit, no connection was made between their diet and their state of well-being. These people trudge up and down the rough mountain paths for anything up to fifty miles a day. Virtually no refined sugar is consumed and their remarkable physical fitness, absence of obesity, cavity-free teeth and longevity are always cited with astonishment.

It is clear that diet plays a tremendous role in maintaining or destroying our health. Don't try to pretend that stress and pollution are the root cause – these never result in dental decay, obesity or blocked arteries – diet, and diet alone, is to blame.

These common dietary mistakes are disease-forming:

- We eat a predominantly acid-forming diet
- We eat a diet too high in animal fats and proteins
- We eat a diet that contains many harmful additives

In addition, we also live incorrectly – this is where stress and pollution come in:

- Too much stress (a certain amount is good for you – the only people who have no stress are in cemeteries)
- Too little exercise
- Too little or too much sunshine
- Too little fresh air

These incorrect dietary and living habits combined, result in many health problems including fatigue, cellulite, excess weight, cravings, binging, insomnia, dark circles under the eyes, pre-menstrual tension, premature ageing, and a host of more serious diseases such as diabetes, heart disease and cancer, to name but a few. I have included such things as fatigue and cravings deliberately, as most people think that these are 'normal'. Believe me, they are not! Sparkling health is normal! So is a glowing complexion, shining hair, and boundless energy!

THE NATURAL BODY CYCLES

Our bodies have natural recurring cycles. We need to sleep every twenty-four hours, although the amount of sleep needed differs from person to person. We also need to eat and drink at regular intervals, and our bowels need to be emptied at least every twenty-four hours (in healthy individuals this is usually first thing in the morning). Women have a monthly cycle in which they ovulate approximately every twenty-eight days.

Scientists now accept that all living organisms have natural cycles. These are sometimes referred to as 'circadian rhythms'. In learning to listen to our bodies, we need to tune into our natural body cycles. A good way to start is by understanding what happens when we sleep. While we are asleep, our bodies automatically step up their repair and cleansing operation. To assist the body in this we need to feed it properly. When, for example, we eat a very heavy evening meal that is also poorly combined, the body is using most of its energy to sort out the mess in the stomach. The result is that the repair, cleansing and rebuilding that should have been done, have been neglected.

We then wake up after eight hours of sleep feeling totally exhausted.

The most obvious benefit that you will enjoy after combining your food properly, is that you'll wake up feeling alive and well rested. Your food will have been digested before you even go to bed and your body can thus carry out it's normal rhythmical chores while you sleep which means that you wake up full of vigour. When you get up in the morning, your body has to eliminate the resultant debris from its repairing and cleansing work. This will be done through the bladder, bowels and other body orifices such as the nose or mouth. Have you ever noticed how a mucus problem is usually worse in the morning and tends to dry up towards lunch-time? This is because your body steps up its elimination first thing in the morning to get rid of the accumulated waste products of the night. This is one of the normal healthy cycles of your body. To facilitate this function, you need to feed the body something that is easy to digest and that won't direct energy away from its cleansing efforts.

This food is fruit.

THE MOST PERFECT FOOD

In a country like South Africa where we have an abundance of fruit available all year round at very reasonable prices, it is surprising that so little fruit is actually consumed. Of the hundreds of people that I have had the opportunity to consult with, either privately or in a seminar environment, very few ate more than one piece of fruit a day and many ate virtually none at all on a regular basis.

But fruit is in fact the most perfect food, designed specifically with man in mind. Now many of you might throw up your hands in protest saying, 'But it is so acidic and I always suffer from digestive problems when I eat fruit'. Let's straighten out the misconceptions right now.

Essie Honiball, who had lived on fruit and nuts for fourteen years and then submitted to a series of extensive tests by Professor B J Meyer (at the time chairman of the Physiology Department at Pretoria University), was found to have alkaline urine. If fruit is indeed acid-forming, this result would not have been possible.

No fruit, not even oranges, causes acid in the body. Some fruit might be acidic before it enters the body, and might digest in a more acid environment than other fruits, but it is never acid-forming in the body or bloodstream unless it is eaten in a wrong combination with other foods. The reason for this is simple – fruit eaten on its own, on an empty stomach, digests in less time than other foods and leaves an alkaline residue in the bloodstream.

Take, for example, the standard way of drinking orange juice. Usually, it accompanies something like toast or a sandwich. Now orange juice (of the freshly-squeezed variety) takes about 15 minutes to one hour to digest and move out of the stomach. Toast or bread needs approximately 2 to 4 hours to move out of the stomach. Imagine what happens next. The juice is mixed up with the bread, through the normal action of the stomach. The orange juice is trapped in the stomach for longer than it should be because of the bread, and the natural sugar in the juice starts to ferment. The acidic value of the orange juice in turn inhibits the digesting ability of the starch digesting enzyme, ptyalin, and so the partially digested starch in the bread starts to ferment. The result ... indigestion! And what gets blamed? The orange juice!

Fruit is so easy to digest because it is what we refer to as a partially digested food. By that it is meant that the nutrients in the fruit are in their most simple form. The sugar in fruit is a simple sugar or monosaccharide. It cannot be broken down any further. Thus it is ready to be absorbed and assimilated directly by the body. By making one meal a day a fruit meal, you'll find that you no longer crave sweets, because you will get enough glucose in your diet. Glucose is one of the most essential nutrients, but it must be taken in an unrefined state – as in fruit.

I used to suffer from severe low blood sugar levels or hypo-glycaemia, with dizzy spells and mood swings ranging to severe depression. When I changed to a high fruit diet all this became a thing of the past. I have since seen that this is always the case in many other people with whom I have consulted. Imagine – no therapy or drugs, just change your diet to one that includes plenty of correctly combined fruit. This brings to mind one particular case where a young woman was institutionalised for mental observation due to extremely severe depression. After various treatments it was finally discovered that her blood sugar level was very erratic. By changing her diet to one high in fruit and vegetables, and by cutting down on animal products, this condition was entirely corrected.

Fruit is truly a complete food. The vitamins and minerals (and that includes calcium and iron in every single fruit) are in a form which is ready to be absorbed and assimilated. The fats in fruit (Oh yes! There is fat in every single fruit – see charts on composition of fruit at the back of the book) are in the form of fatty acids that are ready to be absorbed and assimilated. The protein in fruit (and surprise, surprise, there is protein in every fruit – see tables) is already in its most simple form – that of amino acids – and is ready to be absorbed and assimilated. Now you can begin to understand why fruit digests so easily and requires so little energy for digestion, and why it is the best food to eat when your body is trying to cleanse itself. By eating easily digestible fruit, your body has a lot more energy available to do its cleaning and restoring.

Fruit is in fact the most amazing and perfect food. Not only is it the easiest food to digest, but it is the only food that in its natural state is appealing to all our senses. Fruit looks good. Fruit tastes good. Fruit smells good. Fruit feels good in its natural state. In fact, you can live on fruit alone and be in perfect health. Essie Honiball (*I Live on Fruit*) proved it.

My family has lived on a ninety per cent fruit diet (the other ten per cent being vegetable) since 1985. The change in our health and energy levels has been phenomenal, to say the least. My own mother has followed this programme for nearly as long now and has become a different person. She used to suffer continually from sinusitis, bronchitis, bladder infections, tiredness and a cranky disposition, and she has now become a person who is always positive and in the best of health. In fact, friends and acquaintances who have not seen her for a good many years have asked her, 'Angelique, who did your face-lift?'

It is important to remember that fruit does not do anything to your body, rather your body acts on the fruit that has been taken in. Being the perfect food, it causes very little strain on the body as it contains no toxic or poisonous elements such as those found in virtually every other food.

For example, certain vegetables such as spinach contain oxalic acid, which prevents the absorption of iron. Harmful substances like mustard oil and allicin are usually found together in garlic or onions. Mustard oil is an irritant to the digestive tract and allicin is a natural antibiotic. Simply because it is a natural antibiotic does not make it any better than a pharmaceutically prepared one. An antibiotic is a destructive substance ('anti' means 'against' and 'biotic' means 'life'). It destroys both harmful and friendly bacteria and can disturb the natural intestinal flora or bacteria. Once the balance has been destroyed in the digestive tract, candida albicans or a similar yeast infection could result. Anaemia is another likely problem as vitamin B12 is manufactured in the human body in the small intestine by the natural bacteria or flora which are so easily destroyed by antibiotics.

According to J I Rodale in his book *The Complete Book of Food and Nutrition*, a certain Dr Kalser of the University of Illinois conducted experiments on himself, some medical students and on dogs, in which the effect of onion consumption resulted in anaemia. It was found that the red blood cell and haemoglobin count were starkly reduced with an increased intake of onion.

It has been found that by cooking onion and garlic much of the effect of these properties is reduced. This is one of the reasons why a cooked onion is so much sweeter than a raw one. The stronger the bite of onion or garlic, the more concentrated is the mustard oil and allicin. Mustard oil is also metabolized as thiocyanate in the body, which has been found to suppress the production of the hormone thyroxin from the thyroid gland. This in turn can slow down the metabolism of the body and even result in goitre.

Many grains contain gluten and phytic acid. A great number of people have been found to have an intolerance to gluten which results in various digestive problems, from distension to diarrhoea. Phytic acid, which prevents the absorption of calcium, and gluten are found in all wheat products such as bread, biscuits and cakes.

All animal products contain saturated fats and cholesterol, and red meat also contains uric acid. All of these substances are difficult to break down and therefore place a strain on the body and its functions. Fruit contains none of these.

For the sceptics, hear what our own Professor B J Meyer has to say on the subject in his book *Fruit for Thought* (Prof Meyer is highly respected as the previous chairman of the Physiology Department at Pretoria University): 'By consuming adequate quantities of fruit, a subject can supply his total protein requirements ... it is clear that a fruitarian diet can supply the recommended calcium allowances ... [and that] a balanced fruit diet will supply the recommended daily iron allowances.' A great deal of research has gone into this study and I believe it is a book that every doctor and layman should read. Professor Meyer ends by saying that, '... considering all the pros and cons, it is my firm conviction that from a health point of view a fruit diet, including nuts and

unrefined cereals, has much to be recommended.'
To recap:

- Fruit contains all the nutrients we need
- Fruit allows the body to cleanse itself
- Fruit in its natural state is appealing to all our senses
- All fruit leaves an alkaline residue or end product in the body

Okay! Don't panic, you don't have to become a fruitarian to attain a better level of health. You don't even have to become a vegetarian. You can choose what changes you want to make and how soon you want to make them. Remember, it's your body!

CHAPTER THREE

Food Combining: Does it Work?

What is food combining? In very simple terms it is not eating a concentrated starch with a concentrated protein at the same meal. By sticking to this basic principle you will enjoy a better breakdown and absorption of nutrients, more comfortable digestion and a lot more energy. In this chapter I will explain how and why food combining works and what it can do for you. When you become a 'food combiner' you will know without a doubt that food combining does work and that it can change your life.

Did you know that one of the biggest selling over the counter medications is antacids? Does this not prove that we must be going wrong somewhere and that our eating habits must be less than ideal?

I remember how Mark and I used to suffer from indigestion after virtually every meal. It wasn't that we ate rich meals, it just seemed to be par for the course. Antacid preparations were always in the house and in fact they were a permanent fixture on my shopping list. Whether we went to a barbecue, ate roast chicken and potatoes at home, or had a simple supper of toasted sandwiches or a cheese omelette, we always suffered from indigestion.

Another thing we 'suffered' from was continual tiredness. We slept our weekends away. Saturdays we slept (usually in front of the television) and Sundays we collapsed on the bed after lunch for a couple of hours. Mark used to say sometimes that he felt as if he were sleeping his life away.

The reason I mention these 'symptoms' is that many people 'suffer' from them, and don't realise that this is far from normal. 'Normal' is having boundless energy and never suffering from indigestion or flatulence. 'Normal' is having a digestive system of which you are not even aware. In other words, 'normal' is having no hiatus hernia attacks, no ulcers, no spastic colons or any other digestive-related problem. Over the past years of counselling people about their diets, everyone who has had any digestive problem has been 'cured' by combining foods correctly. There has not been a single person who has not seen or felt a vast improvement in his or her ability to digest food.

Then there were my so-called 'allergy' problems. No amount of medication did anything to relieve my painful symptoms. I had suffered from severe dermatitis or eczema on the palms of my hands for over four years, and my nose had been streaming for over a year. Nothing made any difference and yet I had tried every medical and non-medical avenue open to me: cortisone creams, nasal sprays, homeopathic remedies and vitamin supplements.

It was only when we started combining our food correctly after reading the book *Food Combining for Health*, which is based on the teachings of Dr William Hay, that I experienced immediate relief. My nose stopped running instantly and my hands took about four days to stop itching and to clear up. With our new, properly combined eating regime, indigestion became a thing of the past and our energy levels soared. Two months later we were so well we had almost forgotten what we had felt like before and went back to our old way of eating. The result – instant indigestion, a streaming nose and the next day the little tell-tale blisters appeared between my fingers. We certainly did not need any more proof that food combining worked. But as always, that was not enough for me. I wanted to know how and why it worked.

I started my research by reading as many books on the subject of digestion as I could lay my hands on, going so far as to dig into the Medical Library archives at the University of the Witwatersrand. I read books like, *The Work of the Digestive System* by Professor Pavlov and Charles Griffin (1910). And I was fascinated by the experiments performed on Alexis St. Martin by Dr William Beaumont between 1825 to 1832 and documented in his book. In these experiments Dr Beaumont set out to prove that the stomach did in fact contain a digestive enzyme. He did this by suspending different types of foods on silk threads into the stomach of St. Martin, who had a hole into his stomach from the outside which was caused by a gunshot wound that had not closed up. He would also record any observations made by looking through the hole into the stomach after a meal was consumed. Dr Beaumont recorded the time it took for each meal to digest and from his observations over a few years, it was apparent that the more simple the meal, the easier it was to digest. For example, in one experiment only rice was eaten and this was out of the stomach in one hour. Whereas when potatoes and meat where eaten together, it could take anything from three to six and a half hours to digest. Although these experiments had little to do with food combining (Dr Beaumont had set out to prove that the stomach contains or secretes a digestive enzyme), they did prove that meals consisting of only one type of food took far less time and were more comfortable to digest than a meal that consisted of carbohydrates and proteins together.

Then there were the more detailed books, like *A New Health Era* by Dr Hay and *Food Combining Made Easy* by Dr Shelton. These two books go into the actual physiology of digestion, that is how your digestive system actually works. From my reading I reached the inescapable conclu-

23

sion that if you want complete health, it is essential that you combine your food properly.

Still curious about the subject, I then studied the nutritional course through the Institute of Life Science in Texas. This two-year correspondence course was in fact the most informative and helpful source on the workings of the digestive system.

But the most convincing of all, as far as food combining is concerned, is my own state of well-being as well as that of the hundreds of people I have counselled with digestive related ailments. To date, not one person who has changed to correct combinations has not been helped. From babies to elderly folk, all have experienced a dramatic improvement. To quote Dr William Hay, 'Facts have always discounted theory, and always will; so get the facts for yourself and let others be satisfied with unproved theory'.

So what is food combining or 'The Great Apartheid Diet' as one well-known professor calls it? Very simply, it is not eating a concentrated starch with a concentrated protein at the same meal.

Ah, if it is as easy as that, the sceptics say, if we were not meant to mix starch and protein together, then why do these two occur naturally in all foods? Yes, they do occur naturally in all foods, but they are not found in an equally concentrated form in all foods. The one exception is the legume family (beans, lentils and peanuts), which is high both in protein and carbohydrate content. One thing I have found to be consistent in my research is that everyone I have dealt with experiences digestive discomfort when food from the legume family is consumed, even those with so called 'cast-iron' digestive systems. (We all know the jokes about the effects of baked beans.) Sprouted legumes on the other hand are extremely easy to digest as the carbohydrate to protein ratio changes considerably in the sprouting process.

The second argument favoured by the sceptics is that

early man did not combine his food 'correctly'. My answer to that is that early man ate simply and would not have mixed his foods. In fact we know from research that without refrigeration, early man ate whatever food was most readily available. If he killed an animal to eat, he would have had to consume as much as possible in a relatively short period before the carcass went off. In the absence of a fresh kill, he would quite easily have made a complete meal of the berries, fruit, roots or tubers that he found in abundance. It is unlikely that these two sorts of meals would ever have been eaten at the same time.

But to get back to starches and proteins. Now what is meant by a concentrated starch is usually a food with twenty per cent or more carbohydrate content. Potatoes, rice, bread, noodles, mealies and all grains would fall into this category. (See food combining chart at the back of the book.) These foods need to be chewed very well so that the enzyme ptyalin, which is secreted in the saliva, can start acting on the starch. The ultimate aim is to break these starches down into simple sugars, which is the only way that they can be absorbed into the bloodstream. Very simply, what then happens is that the starch goes into the stomach where it is churned up while the ptyalin continues to act on it. (No additional enzyme which digests starches is secreted in the stomach.) This mixture, called chyme, then passes into the small intestine where further digestion takes places with the aid of amylase or starch splitting enzymes. The simple sugars which result from this breaking-down process, are then absorbed into the bloodstream.

Concentrated proteins are those foods which contain fifteen per cent or more complete protein, such as meat, chicken, fish, eggs and cheese, in fact all animal products other than the fats like butter and cream. Most nuts and seeds also fall into this category. (Refer to chart at the back of the book.) These foods digest in a somewhat different way

25

compared with that of the concentrated starches. They are not acted on by the ptyalin but merely broken down mechanically by the teeth. The chewed protein then passes down to the stomach where hydrochloric acid is stimulated in direct proportion to the amount of protein present. Pepsin, the protein digesting enzyme, is activated by this hydrochloric acid. The pepsin then proceeds with the action of breaking the protein down into amino acids (the building blocks of protein). Further digestion takes place in the small intestine to complete the process. The body can only absorb the protein once it is in this 'broken down' form.

If you were looking at a line graph representing the pH balance at the time of digestion, you would find that protein digests in a more acid environment than starch. Protein prefers a pH level from three down, whereas starch prefers one from four upwards. What happens when you combine the two together is that the hydrochloric acid has a neutralising effect on the more alkaline ptyalin, and in turn this suspends or stops the digestion of the starch midway. The partially digested starches then start to ferment, thus causing the protein to putrefy. The result of this fermenting mess is alcohol, acetic acid (stronger than vinegar) and ammonia. These substances are all poisonous to the body and do end up in the bloodstream, in my case resulting in various 'allergies'. Gas, wind and flatulence are also a result, as is acid indigestion or heartburn. These conditions are ideal for the hiatus hernias and spastic colons to start playing up.

As far back as 1888 Dr James Salisbury, in his research documented in *The Relation of Alimentation and Disease*, found that starches ferment readily in the stomach, resulting in acetic acid being formed. This in turn leads to a variety of symptoms and conditions including headaches, throat congestion, mucus expectoration (this is where my sneezing and runny nose fit in), pains in the heart, sour perspiration, alternate fever and chills (I've found that menopausal women who suffer from hot flushes are 'cured' when they combine properly), and rapid pulse. Dr Salisbury even found that vinegar could, through a chain of events, cause tuberculosis. He also found that vinegar tends to leach phosphorous from the body and stimulates the thyroid gland. As phosphorous is depleted, so in turn is the function of the adrenal system. (The vinegar formed in the stomach through bad combining is no different from any other vinegar. It is a by-product of fermentation. Even so-called health vinegar, such as apple cider vinegar, is a fermented product and could cause the above symptoms. Fresh lemon juice is preferable if you want a tang to your food.)

As a result of the suspension of the digestive process caused by poor combining, food is not broken down completely and the maximum amount of nutrients cannot be absorbed. This results in various deficiencies. Many people with so-called iron deficiencies have had perfectly normal iron levels after only a few weeks of correct food combining.

It can also take double the time to digest a poorly combined meal so that the body has to expend a lot of energy and time on trying to sort out the mess in the stomach. The result is, of course, lack of energy. One of the most immediate benefits of correct food combining is the increase in energy levels. You wake up in the morning feeling rested and refreshed, never groggy or listless. If you have any digestive problems, any allergies or suffer from a lack of energy, the best thing you could do is to try combining your foods correctly for at least a month. I'll guarantee that you will never go back to a badly combined meal again; it is just not worth it.

Now that you know what food combining is, how do you go about implementing it in your diet? Remember the basic rule – do not eat a concentrated carbohydrate or starch with a concentrated protein. You can, however, eat salads or non-starchy vegetables with either of these groups. So if you wanted a sandwich, potatoes, mealies, pasta or rice for a meal, you should not eat a protein like cheese, eggs, fish, chicken, meat or nuts with it. And if you wanted some fish, for example, you should omit starch from the meal. Remember that you can always have any fresh salad or steamed fresh vegetables with either a starch or a protein meal.

This can all be very confusing in the beginning, so let's take it step by step. Let's start with **breakfast**. This should preferably consist of fresh fruit in season. Remember, fruit is the ideal food and you should try to eat at least one fruit meal a day. It is a good idea to have your fruit meal at breakfast simply because you should try to put as little strain on the digestion as possible after the body's rigorous cleansing activities of the night.

Summer fruits, like grapes, are available right up to May or June, but most fruits overlap at the beginning and the end of the seasons. Bananas, pineapples and granadilla are available throughout the year without being put into cold storage. Winter fruits like apples and oranges are often available in summer as they keep well, but fruit that has been in cold storage is not nearly as tasty as fruit in season, and the cores are often black. We try not to eat fruit that is out of season as we don't enjoy it as much when its season eventually comes around. Take apples for example. Athough they are available throughout the year, we eat them in the winter-time so that by the time summer is over, we all look forward to some fresh crunchy apples and we really enjoy them. Also, apples that have been in cold storage tend to be floury.

Here is a simple guide to the seasonal fruits:

SUMMER FRUITS

strawberries	bananas	prunes
cherries	litchis	watermelons
mangoes	peaches	pineapples
apricots	grapes	plums

WINTER FRUITS

oranges	naartjies	minneolas
kiwi fruit	grapefruit	pawpaws
apples	pears	bananas
pineapples	guavas	

Fruit can be eaten whole or chopped in fruit salads or blended in fruit shakes. Although the best way to eat fruit is in it's whole state, sometimes it makes the meal just a little bit more interesting to have a salad or a shake now and again. To make fruit shakes blend any correctly combined fruit (see food combining chart) in a food processor. One of our favourite blends in summer is mangoes and pineapple, but any combination can be delicious. When making a fruit shake, raisins or dates can be added to a sub-acid or sweet fruit combination for extra flavour. Denise Meyer, one of the people that I trained to run a support group in the Springs area, has a wonderful recipe for blending apples and bananas with a teaspoon of macerated dates dissolved in warm water. (Macerated dates are liquidised, vacuum-packed dates. For more on this see *The Natural Way Recipe Book I*.) Nuts can be added to an acid fruit shake.

Now what is all this talk about acid, sub-acid and sweet fruits? Most people find that certain fruits do not digest too comfortably with others and this is simply because of the nutrient structures of the fruits. For example, sweet fruits have a very high sugar content and are digested like starches, whereas acid fruits are digested in a similar way to proteins. Here are some examples of the different fruits and their groupings:

ACID	SUB-ACID	SWEET
gooseberries	apples	bananas
granadillas	apricots	dates
grapefruit	berries	dried fruit

ACID	SUB-ACID	SWEET
guavas	cherries	figs
kumquats	grapes	papinos
lemons	kiwi fruit	pawpaws
limes	litchis	persimmons
naartjies	loquats	prunes
oranges	mangoes	raisins
pineapples	nectarines	sultanas
pomegranates	peaches	
quinces	pears	
strawberries	plums	
tangerines	prickly pears	

Acid fruits combine well with sub-acid fruits, sweet fruits combine well with sub-acid, and sub-acid fruits combine well with both other groups. When eating fruits from two incompatible groups, it is best to separate these fruits by an hour at least.

If you find it difficult at first to have fruit for breakfast, start by adding a piece of sweet fruit to a starch breakfast. An example would be oats with raisins and banana. Sweet fruits and starches digest in a similar pH environment in the stomach, although fruit takes less time. As a transitional meal, this combination can be eaten in the beginning. Fruit on it's own is best, so make this your ultimate aim.

An ideal **midmorning snack** would be more fresh fruit. But if you battle with this in the beginning, a slice of fresh wholewheat toast with butter and avocado or any other salad topping, would do as a transitional snack. Do try to have fruit only if possible.

Lunch could be more fruit if you liked, or a fresh salad with a starch or a protein. (See food combining chart and recipes for ideas.) You might like to try a fresh salad containing tomatoes, lettuce and cucumbers with any non-starch vegetables like broccoli, carrots, peas or cauliflower. These are also referred to as neutral vegetables in the food combining chart at the back of this book. You might want to add one type of starch, like baked potatoes or wholewheat bread, to this. You might prefer to add one type of protein, like fish, to the meal rather than a starch. It is also best not to mix two types of starch or protein at a meal as each type digests far more easily on its own. Also, when we eat more than one type per meal, we tend to overeat.

If you have opted for a light lunch, you might need a **midafternoon snack**, but wait at least three hours after lunch if you had starch or protein, or one to two hours after if you ate a salad or some fruit. A portion of fruit is the ideal snack.

Supper could be the same as lunch, but if you had protein in the day you should not eat another portion for supper. Protein should ideally not be eaten more than once a day, although starch twice a day is not a problem. Remember to include half a cup of raw, unsalted nuts at least three times a week if you are a vegetarian, as many nuts and seeds contain as much protein as fish. It's also a good idea to include an avocado a day as this will prevent any cravings for fatty or greasy food. In fact, if you ever crave fatty foods, eating avocados or nuts will satisfy that craving quite easily.

It is not a good idea to eat after supper as the digestion tends to be less efficient towards the end of the day. It is also not a good idea to go to bed with food in your stomach. Most cooked meals take about four hours to digest and as the body needs to focus it's energy and attention on any healing and repair that needs to be done while you sleep, your last meal of the day should be eaten at least three hours before you retire.

Here follow the times generally taken for food to digest. Bear in mind that digestion depends on many factors, such as how much you eat and what emotional state you are in. If relaxed, the body takes far less time to digest food, but if you are worked up or upset about anything it can take a lot longer. A poorly combined meal can take from four to eight hours and sometimes even longer to digest, depending on the condition of your stomach.

- Fruit properly combined – 15 minutes to two hours
- Fruit badly combined – up to four hours to leave the stomach and during this time it will repeat on you
- Fresh salad with no dressing – one to two hours
- Fresh salad with a dressing that contains oil – up to four hours, longer if the oil is not cold-pressed
- Starch meal – two to four hours
- Protein meal – two to four hours

If you still feel uncertain about how to change to the Natural Way life-style, here are various simple programmes for you to start with. For more detailed information, see the chapters on weight maintenance and making the transition.

OPTION 1

Start your day with properly combined fruit and eat as much of it as you like throughout the morning if you are still hungry. Do not eat fruit with any other food as this combination will ferment in the stomach and cause digestive problems.

Try not to drink tea or coffee during the morning, or try at least to cut back on your intake to start with. Tea and coffee contain both tannin and caffeine, substances which are toxic to the body. Many people who cut these beverages out of their diets from one day to the next, often suffer from withdrawal, experiencing unpleasant symptoms such as headaches, nausea, irritability and 'the shakes'. If you are a regular tea or coffee drinker, start off by reducing your intake gradually. Caffeine can result in insomnia and lumps in the breasts, and it is also potentially harmful to the human foetus. Remember that caffeine is a stimulant that affects the central nervous system, the heart and the kidneys. Tannin is no less toxic and is suspected of causing liver damage. It is best to drink a glass of filtered water or fresh fruit juice when you are thirsty.

Stop eating fruit an hour before lunch to give your stomach a chance to clear. For lunch, have a large fresh salad or a selection of raw vegetables if a salad seems too complicated. (Include one type of starch here if still hungry.)

If you need an **afternoon snack**, try one or two pieces of fruit.

For **supper** start with a large raw salad. Include one type of protein or starch (not to be eaten together) and as many steamed vegetables as you like. Try to eat animal protein no more than four times a week.

OPTION 2

Eat as much properly combined fruit **throughout the day** as you like. Listen to your body – not to your taste-buds. Do not eat if you are not hungry. Make sure to leave at least one hour before supper. For **supper**, follow the suggestions in Option 1.

OPTION 3

Eat fruit at **every meal** and whenever you are hungry. Half a cup of nuts (not peanuts as these are legumes which are extremely difficult to digest, being both high in carbohydrates and protein), unsalted and unroasted, should be eaten at least three times a week. Remember to eat a wide variety of fruit in season. Nuts are best eaten either with a salad or with acid fruits (see food combining chart). Avocados should also be included on the days that you don't eat nuts. Eat one per day if you are watching your weight, but if not three to four can be managed quite easily if you are in the mood.

OPTION 4

This is a combination of the previous three options which can be alternated on a daily basis. Whatever you do, try to have at least one meal a day that consists entirely of fruit.

So there we are. Changing to the Natural Way life-style is not nearly as complicated as you may have feared. At this stage, ask yourself if you suffer from any of the symptoms I have mentioned: indigestion, spastic colon, allergies and lack of energy. If you do, without a doubt, you have everything to gain and nothing to lose if you combine your food correctly. If you are still unsure, try one of these simple programmes for two weeks and then you will have all the proof you need!

CHAPTER FOUR

Case Studies: Changing to the Natural Way Life-style

In this chapter, I have included the most dramatic transformations that various people have experienced when changing their life-styles to a more naturally healthy one. No two people are ever the same; we inherit different metabolisms and our internal organs function at different rates. But each person whom I have counselled, who has managed to stick to the Natural Way programme at least eighty per cent of the time, has experienced a dramatic improvement in health and energy, although some progressed faster than others.

Let's take Melanie for example. Melanie had been a vegetarian for many years but her level of health was quite poor. She came to me slightly overweight and suffering from frequent migraines which struck two to three times a week. She had been on antibiotics for her skin, she had been taking laxatives for fifteen years, as well as antacid fruit salts almost daily for indigestion, the odd tranquilliser for tension, and the occasional paracetamol pain-killer for, as she put it, the odd twitches. She had also resorted to using cortisone cream daily for a troublesome skin rash. After a two-week cleansing programme of just raw fruit, vegetables and nuts (during which time she suffered from detoxification symptoms such as nausea, migraines and general discomfort for about two to three days), Melanie felt like a new person.

Her stomach was working regularly and comfortably for the first time in fifteen years without the aid of a laxative; she had lost weight and came to within her goal weight; her energy levels had improved; she found that she could cope with stress far better than before; and her skin had improved. The indigestion, previously her constant companion, had also disappeared. Everything did not improve overnight, or even in the first two weeks. But during the last nine months, she has stuck to the maintenance programme (a high raw diet with properly combined foods, and no additives) about eighty per cent of the time, Melanie's skin continues to improve as does her general health and well-being.

Dennis was in his sixty-eighth year when he came to see me. As his wife Hanna put it, 'Dennis has been tired since we got married'. Dennis had suffered a heart attack six years previously, was slightly anaemic, overweight and suffered daily from hiatus hernia attacks which were accompanied by vomiting. After six weeks on the maintenance programme together with regular exercising on a rebounder (mini-trampoline), Dennis had his blood tested and found that he was no longer anaemic. His energy levels had improved drastically, and to quote Dennis, 'I have more energy than I've ever had'. The hernia attacks had also become milder and further apart. Now, nearly a year later, Dennis has not had a hernia attack for many months, even though he 'cheats' occasionally. I would like to mention here that Dennis has had the support of his wife Hanna, who joined him in the change to a natural, healthy life-style. I'm sure that without her, he would have battled. Hanna, by the way, has also experienced an improvement in her health and well-being.

Barry, aged thirty-seven years, came to me because his cholesterol was too high (9,2 m/mol). He was also slightly overweight, had low energy and suffered from indigestion. Within a month Barry had lost weight, his cholesterol was down to 6,8 m/mol, his energy had shot up, his general health had improved considerably and his indigestion disappeared.

Terence, aged three, was brought by his mother to see me. Terence had recurring pneumonia. Antibiotics could not clear this up and his mother was told that he would have to be hospitalised as this condition had persisted for six months. His mother was convinced that he would not leave hospital alive. I put Terence onto a cleansing diet for two weeks. For the first two days, all he consumed was water and freshly extracted fruit juice – he wasn't hungry and refused all food. He slept for three hours in the morning and another two to three hours during the afternoon. By the third day he was eating a little fruit and sleeping less. Each day his appetite increased and eventually he was sleeping for only two hours during the afternoon. Two weeks later he was running about, rosy-cheeked and full of beans. For the last two years he has been on the Natural Way programme and he has remained off all dairy products (other than butter) and red meat. He eats no foods containing artificial additives and he is so well that he has not been near a doctor. On the odd occasion when he has eaten incorrectly (at a birthday party for example), his face becomes a bit drawn and his nose might run for two to three days.

Joyce, aged sixty, arrived feeling that life was passing her by. She had no energy and sweated profusely all over her body for no apparent reason. If you could have met Joyce, you would realise how embarrassing this was for her – she was always beautifully dressed and immaculately groomed. Joyce wanted to be off all her medication as well as lose some weight (to be down one dress size, as she put it). Since being on the Natural Way programme for the last one-and-a-half years, she has lost weight and her energy has improved drastically. She no longer gets headaches or takes laxatives, diuretics and appetite suppressants. To put it in Joyce's own words, 'Life is so uncomplicated now'.

Merle came to me in quite a state. She suffered from premenstrual tension accompanied by severe migraines and this would force her to spend two days in bed each month. Part of her recurring problem was that she retained up to three kilograms of water each month. Her doctor had put her on Evening Primrose oil, which caused diarrhoea, a multivitamin and vitamin B6 supplement, but her breasts became enlarged and uncomfortable from this medication. She also suffered from severe pains in one of her kidneys, she felt full and bloated all the time, she had pains in her joints and she had already had polyps and her gall-bladder removed. Merle also craved sweets so badly that she would even get up to raid the kitchen at midnight to try and satisfy her sweet tooth. Although she had been placed on a so-called 'balanced' diet by a dietitian, and exercised almost every day, her problems persisted and her general health remained poor. After placing her on a correctly combined high fruit and vegetable diet, Merle's many problems have cleared up and she has remained in good health for well over a year.

Angelique, who after years of being sick continually with bronchitis, sinusitis and various bladder infections, decided that she was literally sick and tired of taking pills. She showed me copies of three successive monthly medical bills submitted to her medical aid – they were for more than her monthly grocery bill. This was just a sample of her medical history which reflected deteriorating health over many years. Within a month of changing to the Natural Way life-style, she felt like a different person and she has not had a medical bill since. I am sure that her medical aid is thrilled.

There are many others who have changed to the Natural Way programme who prefer to remain anonymous. I think of the fifty-three-year-old man who could not sleep uninterruptedly through the night without his stomach giving him tremendous problems with cramps and wind. He claimed that he went through a packet of antacids in less than a week. He now sleeps through the night and hasn't touched an antacid tablet since changing his eating habits.

Then there is the twenty-three-year-old young man who said that he woke up feeling tired and continued throughout the day in this exhausted state. He could sleep for twelve hours and yet still be tired when he awoke. By cutting out the so-called energy-giving drink that he consumed daily and by increasing the fresh fruit and vegetable content of his diet, he now has boundless energy. As a bonus, his stomach works regularly too.

Many of the people I have counselled do not have 'disgusting' eating habits and in fact most are quite health-conscious. If anything, their eating and exercise programmes are just directionless and they have been confused by the snippets of various health philosophies that they have tried to incorporate into their life-styles. They have all found the Natural Way programme and its principles extremely easy to follow and very rewarding.

I could truly go on and on, citing many more case studies, but the message I'm trying to get across, indeed the purpose of writing this book, is that you can take responsibility for your own health and well-being – and that includes solving any weight problems. It is not difficult at all. Start slowly, make a change, however small, and commit yourself to it. The more you do, the easier it will become and the better you and your family will look and feel. Start now! Remember, your body will sort itself out if you let it.

CHAPTER FIVE

Nutrition: How it Affects The Mind and Emotions

I was speaking to a friend of mine the other day. Margaret has a degree in social work, specialising in psychology, and has worked for one of the top crisis centres in this country for many years. 'Mary-Ann,' she said, 'In all my years of counselling, I've reached the conclusion that ninety-nine per cent of all mental and emotional problems are directly related to the way that people eat and live.' She added that she had yet to come across an individual who was glowing with vitality and health when he or she came for counselling.

The old maxim, you are what you eat, has never been more apt than it is today. We've all moved so far from our natural life-styles, that it is hardly surprising that people have the problems they do. For example, take a look at the high fat diet, which most western societies consume. This can result in a mild form of depression or a pessimistic outlook on life, and then there is the very real risk of cancer! Fat, which is the most complex of foods to break down, results in more blood than normal being diverted from the brain. When body activity and energy is focused on the stomach, which is what happens when too much fat is consumed, the brain does not receive enough oxygen and we become listless and apathetic, our mental processes become slow and confused, and mild depression sets in.

At the opposite end of the scale, drastic dieting is another common problem today, and this can have a devastating effect on the nervous system and often poses serious health risks. One of the main reasons for this is that carbohydrates are usually cut out completely or cut down drastically in most diets. Carbohydrates convert to natural glucose which is the primary nutrient needed for the maintenance of a healthy nervous system. Often the first sign of this deficiency is the extreme irritability that most dieters suffer. Another harmful practice that many diets encourage is the consumption of foods or substances that are extremely low in calories but high in artificial additives. Although they result in rapid weight loss, they can leave the dieter feeling quite terrible and many even cause long-term health problems (see the chapter on additives for more detail). These types of diets discourage the dieter from eating such foods as avocados, bananas, dates and raisins, all of which satisfy many nutritional needs and promote mental and emotional health. It makes absolutely no sense to be allowed relative freedom to consume quantities of low-calorie diet cooldrinks laced with artificial flavourants, artificial colourants and artificial sweeteners (all of which can cause irritability, depression and confusion) while being discouraged from consuming the foods that nature intended us to eat.

Another form of diet that affects the mind and emotions negatively is the so-called high protein diet. This type of diet can result in metabolic disturbances, mental confusion, lack of ability to control emotions, and liver and kidney damage. Apparently the ancient Chinese placed their prisoners on a high protein diet so as to cause a breakdown in emotional resolve and mental health!

Another common dietry mistake is the consumption of refined foods. Processed sugars and grains especially deplete the body of the vital B vitamins. The reason for this is sim-

41

ple. The body needs vitamin B to assimilate sugar but this vitamin is removed or destroyed during processing, resulting in the body robbing itself of the vitamin B it requires. As vitamin B is the anti-stress vitamin, we then find that we cannot cope very well with stress. Eating refined foods can also lead to hyperactivity and hypoglycemia, with the following symptoms: confusion, forgetfulness, poor concentration, emotional outbursts, quick-temperedness, irritability, impatience, depression, weepiness, bad vision (double or blurred), sensitivity to bright light, fatigue, sleeplessness, cold sweats, blackouts, headaches, joint pains, muscle cramping, and cravings for sweets, chocolates and coffee.

You would think that these alarming symptoms, of which there are many sufferers (at least fifty per cent of all women who have been to see me suffer from many of these ailments) would be sufficient to ban refined sugars and grains, together with their products.

The choice is ours. I am certain of one thing, and I have proved it over and over again, and that is that all these symptoms can be cured totally by steering well clear of refined sugars and starches and by changing one's eating habits to include quantities of fresh fruit and vegetables in the diet. I used to suffer from all the above symptoms and at times became quite suicidal. I thought that I had inherited the depression problems from my father's side of the family. Little did I then realise that as health-conscious as I was, the one sweet or chocolate that I ate every other day (and at times more often), affected my blood sugar levels to such an extent that I would look in the mirror and tell myself that I was mad. If it had not been for my desire to find the answers to my problems, with the guidance that I believe could only come from God, and with the support of an extremely loving and caring husband, I might not be here today to tell you this.

It has been extremely interesting to discover that this problem of fluctuating blood-sugar levels along with the accompanying symptoms and craving for sweet things, tends to run in families. Frequently, sufferers also have a history of drinking problems, as did my father and my grandfather before him. But the most amazing thing of all was the discovery that by changing to a diet high in fresh, raw fruits all these symptoms disappeared within a couple of days. I have not suffered from these symptoms for many years, unless I have eaten refined flour or sugar over an extended period of two or three days, which can happen quite easily over Christmas and New Year. As you can see, I am far from perfect but at least I now know why I sometimes feel the way I do, and that makes it so much easier to deal with any problems when they arise.

Let's get back to refined carbohydrates. In 1980, a clinical study appeared in the American journal of Clinical Nutrition, reporting that people who ate too many refined carbohydrates exhibited neurotic tendencies and personality changes. This condition seems to affect adolescents particularly. It was found that the personality changes included sensitivity to criticism, poor impulse control, frequent irritability, hostile behaviour and a tendency to anger easily. It seems that by doing away with refined carbohydrates, we could do away with the generation gap! Other symptoms included sleep disturbance, chronic debilitating fatigue (sounds like Yuppie Flu?), depression, recurrent fevers of unknown origin, abdominal and/or chest pains and headaches.

Isn't this enough evidence to ban refined carbohydrates from your household? When Mark and I changed to this way of eating, I remember telling my children that I would no longer be buying them biscuits or ice-cream as I loved them too much. What about their sense of deprivation, you may ask. Well, the only things you'll be depriving your children of are any one of the above symptoms. In the case of persistent grandparents or friends, read this chapter to them. That should be enough to make them realise that your children are definitely not deprived. The kids won't even miss the 'treats'. Just give them sweet alternatives – dried fruit, especially dates and raisins, are ideal. (See *The Natural Way Recipe Books I* and *II* for plenty of healthy, unrefined sugar-free snacks.)

I could go on and on about the detrimental effects of refined carbohydrates on our mind and emotions, but an excellent book to read on this subject is *Sugar Blues* by William Dufty. This will leave you in no doubt as to how harmful refined foods are.

The link between nutrition and emotional well-being is illustrated in certain studies performed on hyperactive children. It was found that cow's milk produced the same undesirable behaviour just about as frequently as synthetic colouring. Milk has also been found to be a cause of enuresis (bed wetting) in older children. This would no doubt put an emotional and mental strain not only on the child, but on the parents as well. (There is more about milk in the chapter on calcium and dairy products.)

Shortages or deficiencies in vitamins and minerals can also result in mental and emotional problems. Low iron levels can result in impaired judgement and reasoning, and low zinc levels can contribute to anorexia, bulimia and a craving for salt and sugar. Taking supplements is not the answer. These are inorganic, artificial substances which the body cannot metabolise fully. The answer is to eat a diet high in raw food (at least seventy-five to eighty per cent). This way you ensure that you are getting the maximum amount of nutrients and by combining your food properly, you will get the maximum break-down and absorption of these nutrients.

A Dr F M Pottenger conducted some fascinating experiments, initially on cats, to determine the disadvantages of eating cooked food. The results of these experiments are documented in his book, *Pottenger's Cats*. The experiments revealed that cats fed a totally cooked diet of meat, cod-liver oil and pasteurised milk, became irritable. The females

44

became increasingly aggressive, while the males became more docile and their interest in sex slackened or became perverted into abnormal activities between the same sexes. On the other hand, cats eating exactly the same food, but in it's raw state, were in peak condition with none of the above behavioural abnormalities being exhibited. Dr Pottenger then went on to use his 'raw food therapy' on humans with tremendous success.

When food is cooked, many nutrients are either partially or totally destroyed. The water soluble vitamins B and C are especially vulnerable and are destroyed in foods which are cooked in water, as are the fat-soluble vitamins A, D, E and K when food is fried. Cooking also changes the structure of certain nutrients, resulting in difficulty in assimilation by the body. For this reason, it is best to steam any foods that you might want cooked as this method tends to destroy the least nutrients.

So what kind of diet encourages mental and emotional well-being?

- A diet that supplies all the necessary nutrients
- A diet that is free from non-foods or refined junk foods that will rob the body of nutrients
- A diet that is free from all toxic substances such as alcohol, cigarettes and artificial additives and flavourants
- A diet that is high in raw food content

If you follow the Natural Way programme as outlined in this book, you will be sure that your diet encompasses all the above criteria. And you will experience not only mental and emotional well-being, but the physical well-being that goes with it. You will be in control of your mind and emotions and the improvement in your overall quality of life will be worth the small sacrifices and discipline involved.

CHAPTER SIX

Calcium, Osteoporosis and Dairy Products: Is There a Connection?

The connection between calcium and dairy products is something that had confused me for many years. Firstly, I discovered that whenever I ate or drank any dairy products, especially milk, I would get a terrific build up of mucus and I seemed to be spending my life clearing my throat or blowing my nose. I also discovered that when I discontinued the dairy products, within a couple of days the mucus would be gone. The same can be said for all three of my daughters. Melissa's tonsillitis would clear up, Marie-Claire's nose would stop running and Meredith's ear infection would clear up – until I introduced the dairy products again.

Now you might ask, how could I have been so stupid? Well, it was quite simple. I believed all the old wives' tales about calcium and dairy products. You know the sort, 'You can't cut dairy products out of your diet or you'll suffer from osteoporosis' (brittle bones due to the loss of minerals, especially calcium). Yet I kept coming across an article or a book telling me that I'd be far better off if I cut dairy out of my diet completely. So I decided to investigate.

Firstly, what did those people advocating dairy products have to gain? Well, it made economic sense for the Dairy Board to wax lyrical about the tremendous health benefits of consuming their product. And then there were certain members of the medical profession who got quite worked up about the need for dairy products in the diet. Perhaps they were just misguided or perhaps they saw themselves losing a lot of revenue from those poor people suffering from ear infections, tonsillitis, asthma and sinusitis.

Then I looked at those suggesting that I eliminate dairy products from my diet. What did they have to gain? Nothing! I wasn't being sold a special supplement to make up for all the calcium that I wouldn't get from milk, and they weren't getting any business from my family as we were no longer sick.

But the bearers of bad news did not stop. Regardless of the fact that my children never had even the slightest sniffle and were pictures of glowing health, the comments came fast and furiously, 'My doctor says you'll all get rickets.' (Rickets, by the way, is due to a lack of vitamin D or sunshine rather than to lack of calcium.) 'My sister-in-law is a dietitian and she says your children won't grow properly.' (All three my girls are in the top ten per cent for their height years after discontinuing dairy products.) The best was when Melissa came home from school one day to tell me, 'Mommy, my health teacher says I'll get holes in my teeth if I don't drink milk, and I'm the only one in the class without any fillings!'

So what are the facts? It's a fact that in the countries that have the highest incidence of dental decay (which, by the way, is classed as a disease) and osteoporosis, also have the highest intake of dairy products. In countries with the lowest intake of dairy products there is also the lowest incidence of these diseases. I have also seen that many of the women who seek help from me, regardless of the fact that they take in vast quantities of dairy products, have not yet been able to stop the loss of calcium from their bones.

It should be quite obvious that dairy products will not prevent calcium from being lost from the body, and nor will it cure calcium deficiencies. Why? Well, to start with, we need an organic source of calcium. This is not available in milk products as they have been pasteurised or heated to destroy bacteria, and in the process the calcium becomes inorganic. We can absorb inorganic calcium but our cells cannot utilise it very efficiently. Secondly, at about the age of two or three, when we have most of our teeth, we stop secreting an enzyme called lactase which breaks down the sugar in milk. We also don't secrete an enzyme that breaks down the protein in cow's milk. Calves have this enzyme – it's called rennin. This brings me to another point about milk. Cow's milk is perfectly designed for calves and human milk is perfectly designed for humans. Humans are perfectly designed to be weaned at the age of two, and yet we refuse to be weaned, believing that we need these milk products to be healthy.

So, you may well ask, from where are we going to get our calcium? Well, from the food that we as humans were designed to eat – fruit, vegetables, nuts and seeds. According to the National Research Institute for Nutritional Diseases of the South African Medical Research Council, every single fruit, vegetable, nut and seed contains calcium (refer to charts at the back of the book). According to *Fruit for Thought* by Professor Bernard J Meyer (professor of physiology and past chairman of the Department of Physiology at the medical faculty of the University of Pretoria), a fruitarian diet can supply the daily recommended calcium requirements.

Now, the aim of this book is not to convert everyone to fruitarianism (although you would be far better off!), but to make you aware of the very important role that fresh fruit should play in your diet, and to demonstrate that cow's milk is not vital to your health. Some recent research completed by Cornell University together with the aid of Chinese researchers and Oxford University, shows that dairy calcium is not needed to prevent osteoporosis. The research involved the dietary life-styles of 6 500 Chinese who consume no dairy products whatsoever. According to Dr Campbell, who headed the project, sufficient calcium is obtained from the vegetables and grains that make up the bulk of their diet. Osteoporosis is uncommon in China and so is dental decay.

Closer to home, Professor Marius Barnard, at a convention held at Sun City on 18 May 1989 said, 'Humans must be the only mammals who continue to provide milk in their diet after being weaned,' and 'Man has become a walking disaster because we eat like pigs!'

Now the question still remains, why do we suffer from such a high incidence of osteoporosis and dental decay? Does milk cause it? Not necessarily, although it could be a contributing factor. One of the main reasons that our systems lose calcium is because of our highly acid-forming diet. Certain foods, such as all animal products and, to a lesser degree, all grains, have an acidic reaction on our blood. In other words, meat, chicken, fish, eggs, milk, cheese, yoghurt, wheat, rice, maize and barley, are all acid-forming or leave an acid ash in the bloodstream. When our diet is more than 25% acid-forming, the body needs to neutralise the acidity in some way. The reason it has to do this, is that the blood is slightly alkaline (± 7.35–7.45 on the pH scale) and if the blood were to become acidic, we would die. Rather than allow this to happen, the body utilises its neutraliser or buffer, and the main 'ingredient' of this buffer system happens to be the mineral calcium. How does the body obtain calcium? It derives it from the bones and teeth resulting in dental decay and osteoporosis. (Way back in 1974, Anand and Linkswiler showed that a high protein intake resulted in the body losing calcium, and that a low protein intake facilitated calcium retention.)

Let's take a look at the average Westerner's way of eating, and how this affects calcium levels.

Wake up – tea or coffee with milk and sugar. All are acid-forming!

Breakfast – this usually consists of either one or all of the following: toast, bacon and egg, cereal, cooked porridge, muesli, French toast, toasted cheese or mince on toast. All are acid-forming! Fruit is sometimes eaten with these foods and although fresh, uncooked fruit is normally alkaline-forming, when eaten with other foods it tends to ferment in the stomach causing acidity.

Mid-morning snack – sandwiches, biscuits, sweets or chocolate and tea or coffee. All are acid-forming!

Lunch – an average non-business meal would consist of sandwiches, margarine, peanut butter, jam, toasted sand-wiches, cheese, tuna, hotdogs or hamburgers. All are acid-forming! A bit of salad or a slice of tomato is sometimes included in some lunches. Although all salad and vegetables are alkaline-forming, once you combine your food incorrectly you end up with an acidic mess in your stomach.

Mid-afternoon – biscuits, some type of pastry or sugar-based food with tea or coffee. All are acid-forming!

Supper – meat, chicken or fish, rice, pizza, pies, macaroni and cheese or spaghetti. All are acid-forming! Salads and veg-etables are often included in this meal and these are all al-kaline-forming. But this is usually followed by dessert which, in any form, is acid-forming. So too is the last cup of tea and coffee of the day. Add to this cigarette smoke and air pollution, and the acid-forming percentage is pushed up even further.

You can see by this example of the way the average person eats, why it is that we have such a high incidence of dental decay and osteoporosis. (Remember that the body uses its own stores of calcium in the teeth and bones to neutralise the acidity.)

How do we overcome this problem? Simply by returning to a more natural way of living and eating. To do this we need to make sure that our diet is seventy-five per cent alkaline-forming. And the way to achieve this is to:

- Start each day with fresh fruit and to continue eating fruit during the course of the morning when hungry
- Make sure that all meals are properly combined
- With each meal, other than fruit meals, enjoy a large fresh salad with as many other vegetables (raw or steamed) as you can manage
- Avoid tea and coffee if possible, or limit to one cup per day
- Try not to eat protein more than once a day
- Snack only on fresh or dried fruit or raw vegetables

Remember that many other habits are also acid-forming, such as cigarette smoking, drinking alcohol and the use of drugs (including medication of any kind).

Remember too that if any member of your family suffers from any mucus-related symptoms or diseases, the best thing you can do is to eliminate all dairy products from the diet. You definitely will never suffer from calcium deficiency if you follow the guide-lines set out above.

If for some reason you are not too confident about eliminating dairy products from your Natural Way programme, have your blood tested regularly. This way you will be able to monitor your calcium levels and enjoy peace of mind!

CHAPTER SEVEN

Protein and Meat:
Is There a Difference?

Most people think that protein and meat are one and the same thing, and that without any animal flesh in your diet you won't be getting any protein. Before we examine this misconception, let's first find out what protein is, why we need it and how much we need.

Protein is made up of twenty-three amino acids, eight of which our body cannot manufacture and which it needs to obtain from our diet. Amino acids are the building blocks of protein. They formulate the different types of protein our bodies need, of which there are many thousands. Originally it was taught that we need to take in the eight essential amino acids at each meal. But in recent years it has been found that we have an 'amino acid pool' from which our body 'draws' or into which it 'deposits' amino acids as it needs them. This amino acid pool is in the blood, the liver and the cells. If you eat too much of one type of amino acid it is deposited in the amino acid pool. Then when there is too little of any of the amino acids in the food you eat, the body withdraws what it needs from the amino acid pool. You can begin to understand where the idea of bacon and eggs for breakfast, the cheese for lunch and the meat for supper originates, especially considering that it was thought that animal products were our only reliable source of protein. We now know that even on a fruit diet adequate amounts of protein can be supplied to the body (refer to the charts at the back of the book).

This gets me back to how much protein is needed. In his book *Nature of Protein Requirements*, N S Scrimshaw is of the opinion that the average young man leading a fairly active life needs only 30 grams of protein per day. This is far lower than the generally accepted 'norm'. *Guyton's Textbook of Medical Physiology (7th edition)* states that the body loses about 20 to 30 grams of protein per day, 'therefore to prevent a net loss of protein from the body one must ingest a minimum of 20 to 30 grams of protein each day,' although '... to be on the safe side, 60 to 75 grams is recommended.'

An easy way to work out your protein needs is to make sure you get one gram of protein for every two kilograms of body weight. We need protein mainly for growth and repair, and the period that we grow the fastest is during the first six months of our lives. During this time nature has provided us with the most perfect food; mother's milk. The average percentage of protein in this milk is a mere 1,6% – less than in the average fruit! As adults we need protein only for repair (especially as we often have damaging habits like smoking and drinking). But the average adult in western society consumes far more than is needed with the result that calcium is lost from the body in the urine. (Remember calcium is used to neutralise the acidity caused from too much protein in the diet.) The danger, in this society, therefore, is not that we don't get enough protein, but ensuring that we don't get too much. Surprisingly enough, all fruit and vegetables contain protein, with many of them, like bananas, tomatoes, carrots, avocados and nuts, containing all eight essential amino acids. The protein content in these foods is:

    1 medium banana – 0,8g
    1 medium tomato – 2,2g
    1 medium carrot – 0,8g

1 small avocado – 2,5g
1 cup almonds – 24,18g
1 cup cashews – 25,08g

(For additional information on the nutritional content of fruit and vegetables, see the tables at the back of the book.)

T Colin Campbell, a nutritional biochemist from Cornell University, has performed the most up to date and most comprehensive nutritional research. This involved documenting the dietary habits of one hundred Chinese people from sixty-five different regions over a period of time. The research done by Dr Campbell and his colleagues has been ongoing since 1983. By 1990 some of the conclusive results showed that, to quote from the actual research, 'Consumption of a lot of protein, especially animal protein, is also linked to chronic disease. Americans consume one third more protein than do Chinese and 70% of American protein comes from animals, while only 7% of Chinese protein does. Those Chinese who eat the most protein, and especially the most animal protein also have the highest rates of "diseases of affluence", like heart disease, cancer and diabetes.' According to the research, when animal protein is ingested, cholesterol comes with it as part of the package. All animal products contain cholesterol including so-called low-fat dairy products, fish and chicken. I mention this here as many people are of the opinion that only eggs contain cholesterol. No fruit or vegetable, however, has the ability to manufacture cholesterol as all animals do. Therefore no plant food contains cholesterol. The research conducted by Dr Campbell also shows that those who consume the most protein and have the highest cholesterol levels, are not only prone to the 'diseases of affluence', but also show a tendency to cancer of the colon. Dr Campbell concludes that, 'We're basically a vegetarian species and should be consuming a wide variety of plant foods and minimizing our intake of animal foods.'

It is clear from Dr Campbell's research that man is a lot healthier if he consumes very little or no animal products. Quoting from my favourite authority on the subject, Professor Meyer, in this book *Fruit for Thought*, 'By consuming adequate quantities of fruit, a subject can supply his total protein requirements.' And 'considering all aspects; a fruitarian diet can easily supply the protein requirements of the human body, as well as the energy requirements, provided that it contains suitable quantities of avocado and/or nuts.'

It makes a lot of sense to stick to a high fruit and vegetable diet, especially considering the antibiotics and hormones that are fed to animals. These ensure that they grow quicker so that the farmers can realise a speedy profit. It is now thought that this hormone-laden meat could be responsible for our children maturing at a much younger age than those of earlier generations. (With earlier maturation comes earlier degeneration.) Then there is the sodium sulphite, a chemical substance which is used on red meat to retain it's natural colour. Scientific research shows us that this substance could aggravate or even trigger asthma attacks and any other respiratory tract problems. In processed meats (which, by the way, are made of the left-over snouts, udders, lips, eyes and ears), sodium nitrate and nitrite are used as colourants and preservatives. The question here, say the scientists, 'is not whether it causes cancer, but how much it causes'. Under the circumstances, it seems that animal proteins are not such a wise choice.

If you still enjoy eating meat, then as a rule fish is best, then free range chickens, then venison (no hormones or antibiotics) and then red meat that has not been treated with sodium sulphite. Ask your butcher for untreated meat. Try not to eat animal protein more than once a day, in other words if you have had some fish for lunch, don't eat more protein for supper. Have a properly combined starch meal instead.

If you are a vegetarian or if you plan to move in that direction, then you should include in your diet half a cup (or 100g) of raw, unsalted nuts three times a week or at least one or two avocados. Remember that peanuts are classed as legumes rather than nuts. They are difficult to digest as they are high in both protein and starch with a tendency to ferment easily in the stomach. When eating nuts, remember to combine them as a protein, although they can, on occasion, be combined with acid fruit.

So what about protein in the diet? It is clear that you do not have to eat animal flesh or products to get your daily protein requirements. Nor do you have to eat a complete protein at each meal provided that you are on a properly combined, high raw diet. If, however, you enjoy meat, fish and poultry, then try not to eat these more than once a day, keeping your intake of red meat down to a maximum of three times per week. And remember that in the society in which we live, there is more chance of getting too much protein, with the resultant kidney damage and loss of calcium, than there is of getting too little!

CHAPTER EIGHT

Fats: Are They Needed?

Yes, fats are needed in your diet, indeed they are essential. But the majority of us not only consume far too much on a daily basis, but also the wrong kinds of fats on top of it.

Firstly, fat is needed as a source of heat and energy in the body. Our body temperature needs to be constant no matter what the weather, and we need energy at the most basic level just to keep the heart beating. Secondly, fat is also needed for padding and insulating the organs and nerves. I'll never forget how uncomfortable it was to sit after the first fourteen-day fast I completed – I simply had insufficient padding and found it more comfortable to stand until my fat reserves had been rebuilt. Thirdly, fats play an essential role in the diet; they are needed to help with the absorption of the fat soluble vitamins A, D, E and K. I found it very interesting that all fruit (yes, even watermelon contains fat – see tables at the back) and vegetables contain vitamin A along with fat – wise Mother Nature has made sure that the vitamin A is able to be absorbed and assimilated due to the presence of fat. Fourthly, fats are a source of essential fatty acids. These are needed for the proper functioning of the endocrine system (especially the adrenal glands), production of hormones, growth and reproductive activity, for production of vitamin B12 in the intestines, and to help make calcium and phosphorous more available. Lack of, or insufficient, fatty acids can result in skin disorders, gallstones, loss of hair, impaired growth and reproductive function, and kidney, prostate and menstrual disturbances.

There is absolutely no need to add more fat to your diet if you have any of these problems, rather a shift from processed, heated fats to natural unheated fats is often all that is required. All nuts, seeds, avocados and raw sweet corn contain all the essential fatty acids. These can be consumed quite comfortably, at least one of them each day. Now, before you throw up your hands in horror about cholesterol in nuts and avocados, let me reassure you. There is no cholesterol in any plant. Cholesterol is produced only in animals, so all animal products (not only eggs) contain a certain amount of cholesterol.

But according to a Dr Henry Beiler the real problem with fats is not so much the cholesterol content, but whether or not the fat has been heated. He says that overeating of fats and oils, as long as they are in their natural state, cannot cause arterial disease. The body merely stores the excess as fat. It is only when we consume unnatural fats (such as tea and coffee creamers) or natural fats which have been altered by being overheated, that the trouble arises. Why are heated fats so bad for us? Quite simply, we do not have enzymes which are able to break down fats heated over about 100°C. It is for this reason that frying is out of the question from a health point of view as fried fats are heated way over 100°C. Adding a bit of butter to vegetables after they have been cooked poses no threat, as the temperature at which the butter melts is way below 100°C. Included in the category of natural fats that have been heated are all the oils that have been pressed or extracted from seeds, such as sunflower, sesame and olive oil. Unless the label states that it has been 'cold pressed', all oils are heated numerous times in the extraction process. All margarines are heated during processing and even butter used in baking a cake or biscuits is also heated way above 100°C.

We have been led to believe by the oil, margarine and advertising companies, that all vegetable fats are better than any animal fat. But is this in fact true? Let us compare the relative merits of butter and margarine. Butter is not heated during processing, in fact you can make your own butter if you like, simply by beating cream past the thick stage to when it separates. You then rinse the fatty part that is formed and pour off the watery part. You then have unsalted butter. If you prefer salted butter, just add a little salt. According to the Dairy Board, the amount of salt in butter is about two per cent. Occasionally annato (a natural colouring extracted from a tree) is used. The body is capable of handling this fat quite comfortably. Whereas the same cannot be said for margarine which is heated several times before it eventually reaches our tables.

Here is a brief summary of how oils and margarines are manufactured in South Africa. This method is approved internationally, according to the oil companies. However, they neglect to mention that approval does not necessarily mean that these products are good for you! The seeds from which the oil is extracted, are first decorticated or husked. They are then subjected to steam so that the cells will rupture with ease and thus release more oil. The seeds are then dried, using a heat process once again. At this stage, the seeds pass through an expeller, leaving about twenty per cent of the oil in the caked seed. Hexane, a benzine derivative, is now percolated through the leftover seed-cake, in order to extract the remaining oil. The oil is then filtered and neutralised with caustic soda. Bleaching follows at this point, by using bleaching earth and by heating the oil in a vacuum. Here, the oil is winterised or cooled to a very low temperature. This is to filter out harmless, natural wax crystals. Apparently the housewife does not like the milky appearance the crystals give the oil. Under vacuum the oil is heated yet again, this time to between 220° and 290°C, to render the oil odourless. Apparently we would find the natural smell of the seeds offensive. To this insipid, odourless concoction, colourant is now added. Unless of course we prefer to buy a 'light' oil, then the paler the better. (As if calories had anything to do with colour!) The oil is now ready for bottling to be sold to us as salad or cooking oil.

In the manufacturing of margarine, the oil goes through all the above processes and is then hydrogenated in the presence of a nickel catalyst. This is to ensure that this denatured, destroyed oil can be spread like butter. But that's not all! Whey, a watery fluid separated from milk, is now added, and so too are butter flavouring and the preservative sodium benzoate. This particular preservative has been found to result in foetal damage and respiratory problems such as asthma and bronchitis. Yet despite this questionable process and equally questionable product, we are constantly told that margarine is healthier for the heart than butter!

Let's face it, genuine old-fashioned butter and cold-pressed oils just have to be better. I'd like to add here that this should not give you license to over-indulge in cream and butter as any fat in excess is not good for you. As a family, we try to avoid eating fat more than once a day. For example, we would try not to put an oil dressing on a salad containing avocado. The National Cancer Association states that too much fat in the diet can cause cancer, and although they don't state whether the research was done using heated or unheated fats, there does seem to be evidence though that heated fats are the culprit.

When it comes to fats, the consumer is frequently baffled by the terms 'saturated', 'unsaturated' and 'polyunsaturated'. I sometimes think that these terms are thrown at us from all angles, in the hope that we will become so confused that we will believe all the advertising claims about fats and buy the latest product of the moment. I hope to be able to clear up some of this confusion.

Saturated fats are fats which are solid at room temperature. They are found mostly in animal products like meat, chicken, eggs, cheese, milk and butter. Saturated fats are also present in coconuts. 'Saturated' simply means that these fats do not have the ability to form nutrient-bonding in the body. In other words, they are usually only empty calories that contribute to a fat build-up or weight gain in the body. Saturated fats, when from an animal source, are always accompanied by cholesterol. (Remember that plants are unable to manufacture cholesterol.) Cholesterol, as we all know, contributes to heart disease when consumed in excess. Although it is important to remember that cholesterol is manufactured by our bodies and serves a very useful purpose, namely to manufacture cell membranes, nerve tissue, hormones and bile acids used to digest food, our bodies produce the right amount of cholesterol for healthy maintenance in these areas. By consuming a diet high in fresh raw fruit and vegetables and following the Natural Way principles outlined in this book, you will be able to maintain the correct cholesterol blood levels that result in optimum health. (Refer to the chapter on case studies for examples of how to lower your cholesterol level.) It might be interesting to note here that it has now been found that the research done on the effects of oat bran on cholesterol levels was incorrectly concluded, and that oat bran is not in fact the answer to a cholesterol problem. A change in the general diet will do far more to rectify this problem.

Unsaturated fats are fats which, in their chemical structure, have open links. This structure enables them to combine easily with various nutrients and they are therefore put to use easily in the cells. Unsaturated fats are found mainly in all nuts, seeds and avocados, and all fruit and vegetables contain small quantities of this type of fat.

Polyunsaturated fats are those which have large numbers

of fatty acids which in turn have open linkages and are therefore also easily utilised by the cells. These are also found in all fruit, vegetables, nuts and seeds.

Monounsaturated fats are fats which have a single fatty acid with open linkages, and are found in all fruit and vegetable sources.

Saturated fats, because of their inability to be put to use by the body, are usually classed as the 'bad' fats, and unsaturated, monounsaturated and polyunsaturated fats are classed as the 'good' fats. As there are generally no saturated fats in plant foods, this is even more reason to step up your intake of fruit, vegetables, nuts and seeds. The recommended fat allowance is generally thirty per cent of your daily food intake, although the research done in China by Cornell and Oxford Universities as previously mentioned in this book, indicates that a maximum of twenty per cent is sufficient, although ten to fifteen per cent is best. A diet high in fresh vegetables, fruit, nuts and seeds would supply all your body's needs for fat.

To summarise, fats are needed by the body, but make sure that you stick to the right kinds of fat. There is no need to add additional fat to your diet as all fruit, vegetables, nuts and seeds contain the correct sorts of fat. Ensure that these foods make up the bulk of your diet. And when it comes to making healthy choices for your body, butter is better than margarine.

CHAPTER NINE

Additives:
The Invisible Enemy

Additives are the body's invisible enemy – invisible because we can't see them, and we are not even alerted to their presence as they are often not listed on food packaging.

I feel very strongly about being given a choice – if we choose to consume, or not to consume, foods containing certain additives, the decision should rest with us. But we should at least have the right to know exactly what we are eating so that we can be in a position to choose intelligently and correctly. Here everyone can take a cue from Woolworths, who do their best to list all ingredients on the packaging. This practice does not automatically stamp the product as 'good', but it does give you, the consumer, 'the right of first refusal'.

Additives seem to affect so many people, especially children, adversely. But nine times out of ten, most people don't know that the additives are to blame. I believe that every home should have a book on additives on the bookshelf. An excellent one is *Additives – A Guide for Everyone* by Eric Milstone and John Abraham.

In this chapter, I have compiled a list of the most common additives and their possible side-effects. 'Food Additives', something you see frequently on packaging these days, refers to chemicals added deliberately during industrial food processing. Because, more often than not, these substances are preservatives and colourants, the manufacturers believe that using these chemicals enhances their product and makes it easier to sell. Additives are sometimes identified by the letter E, which is followed by a number. The letter E is the standard identification code in Europe for additives and there are currently over four thousand additives in use internationally. Each additive has an 'E' number, and this number alone is often listed on the packaging instead of the name of the substance, so beware! For this reason it is a good idea to keep an additive book handy. Although the amounts of additives used by manufacturers are 'legal', the accumulative and combined effect of these substances can cause a tremendous amount of unnecessary pain and suffering.

Time and time again I have come across a man or woman suffering from recurring severe migraines. These people are usually at their wits' end as they have been for every sort of test imaginable, including brain scans. After taking one look at their diets I found, without exception, that one of the following additives was the cause of the trouble: caffeine, monosodium glutamate (MSG), and in some cases, the artificial sweetener aspartame. In other cases where recurring bronchitis is the problem, when the additive sulphur dioxide is removed from the diet, the bronchitis disappears 'miraculously'.

Here follows a more detailed description of the most common additives, where they are found, and what they do.

THE COLOURANTS

Tartrazine – E 102

Tartrazine is a bright yellow coal tar dye, commonly found in many sweets with colours ranging from cream to yellow to orange to green. Tartrazine is generally recognized to be responsible for a wide range of allergic and intolerant symptoms, including hyperactivity in children, asthma, migraine headaches, and skin rashes. According to some research, tartrazine is also suspected as a possible cause of cancer. Its use is prohibited in Norway and Finland and restricted in Sweden. We often make the mistake of thinking that if a food is tartrazine-free, it is safe to consume, regardless of what other additives it may contain.

Annato – E 160 (b)
This is a natural yellow colouring extracted from the annato tree and used to colour cheese and butter. The Dairy Board claims that it is totally harmless, but there is evidence that it can provoke symptoms of intolerance in people who are susceptible to urticaria (hives) or angioneurotic oedema (a severe condition of hives or a bad skin rash).

Aluminium – E 173
Used as a silver colourant, aluminium is also found in tea (though not herbal teas). Aluminium pots can oxidize and contaminate the food during the cooking process and can then be absorbed into the body. There is evidence that this metal plays a part in the onset of Alzheimer's disease or senility.

THE PRESERVATIVES
Sodium Benzoate – E 211
Sodium benzoate is used in all South African margarines, and in some dried fruits, cooldrinks and bottled sauces. In all related studies, levels of consumption have been found which provoke ill-health including (in some cases) foetal damage, hyperactivity, asthma and urticaria.

Sulphur Dioxide and the Sulphiting Agents – E 220 and E 227 (including Sodium Sulphite)
These substances are commonly found in all dried fruit other than the 'dark' dried fruit like dates, raisins, unbleached

sultanas and prunes. If the dried fruit retains its original colour, if the dried peaches are bright yellow for example, then more often than not it has been treated with sulphur dioxide. It is also one of the most widely-used preservatives as it is readily available and inexpensive. It is also found in beer, wine, sausage meat, soups, sauces and dried vegetables. Sodium sulphite is used on red meat to retain the red, fresh appearance. Sulphur dioxide and sodium sulphite can reduce levels of calcium as well as enhance the carcinogenic (cancer forming) action of any known carcinogen. It also destroys vitamin Bl, and can cause nausea and headaches. It can provoke asthma attacks, eczema, hypertension and ulcers. I have found that in several cases it has caused severe coughing in children, which in some instances had been diagnosed as bronchitis by their own doctors.

Sodium Nitrite and Nitrate – E 250 and E 251
These substances are found in virtually all processed meats, bacon, polony and viennas. They interfere with the mechanism for distributing oxygen around the body and they also combine with amines (basic chemicals found in our food) to produce nitrosamines, which are among the most carcinogenic substances ever identified. The question, say the scientists, is not whether they cause cancer but how much cancer they cause.

Acetic Acid – E 260
Acetic acid is the main ingredient of vinegar and is thus found in all bottled mayonnaises, dressings, pickles and sauces. It is used both as a flavourant and a preservative. It is a corrosive and toxic substance which irritates the tissues and can damage the central nervous system, the kidneys and the liver. Remember that acetic acid is a by-product of fermentation of food in the stomach, frequently the result of poor combining.

Calcium Propionate – E 282

This is used widely in breads, ranging from white loaves right through to wholewheat and rye. It can cause gastro-intestinal symptoms similar to a gallbladder attack, and it may also be a cause of migraines. Calcium propionate destroys the enzyme that enables us to assimilate calcium. Imagine a more questionable combination than margarine on bread! So use butter and bake your own bread.

THE SWEETENERS

Sorbitol – E 420

Sorbitol is used mainly as an artificial sweetener. Formerly presumed safe, recent research shows that there is the possibility of its being carcinogenic, causing, in particular, bladder tumours. It can also produce diarrhoea. Sorbitol is not permitted in any baby foods.

Aspartame – No E number given as yet

Aspartame is also marketed as Nutrasweet, Canderel and various other brand names. Independent scientists claim that aspartame causes mental retardation, brain lesions and neuroendocrine disorders (disorders to do with the nervous and endocrine systems) thus affecting the thyroid, pituitary and adrenal glands, and the ovaries and testes. In laboratory experiments, lesions were produced in the uteruses of rats. According to a Professor Wurtman, it may also disturb brain function in a variety of ways resulting in epileptic seizures. Further research shows that chronic brain damage may be caused when aspartame is consumed in combination with monosodium glutamate. Dr Gale from Searle SA, the manufacturers of Canderel, assures me that these conclusions are unfounded. However, I have yet to see the results of long term research, conducted over at least two generations, which prove safety.

Saccharin – No E number given as yet

Saccharin has been found to cause cancers in laboratory tests, particularly cancer of the urinary tract. There has been much controversy surrounding this product over the past century, but the fact remains that it is carcinogenic and mutagenic.

MISCELLANEOUS ADDITIVES

Monosodium Glutamate – No E number given as yet

Also known as MSG, this flavour enhancer stimulates the taste-buds which causes them to become inflamed and more sensitive. This deceives us into thinking that foods have more flavour than they really do. MSG is found in packet soups, aromat, fondor, stock-cubes, sauces and other artificial flavourants. In fact, almost every processed food contains this chemical. MSG affects the chemistry of the brain, and can cause acute discomfort to the body, including headaches, and respiratory and muscle tightness.

Caffeine – No E number given as yet

Caffeine is found in coffee, cocoa, tea, chocolate and cola drinks. (It is not usually found in herbal teas.) It is a flavouring agent that acts as a stimulant, in turn affecting the central nervous system, the heart and the kidneys. Consumption can result in nervousness, anxiety, irritability and insomnia. There is strong evidence that caffeine may contribute to the formation of breast lumps. It has also been shown that coffee drinkers are more likely to suffer from heart disease.

This is by no means a comprehensive list of additives, and is in fact merely the tip of the iceberg. It does, however, give you an idea of the additives found most commonly in our foodstuffs. For more information read *Additives – A Guide for Everyone* by Eric Milstone and John Abraham.

IRRADIATION

An additive not generally regarded as such is irradiation or radurization. Irradiation is a preservation treatment, using very large doses of ionizing radiation, that produces a change in food in order to ensure a longer shelf-life. The materials used to irradiate food are cobalt 60 or cesium 137, common nuclear waste products. Irradiation is not new and has been around without our knowledge since 1916 when the first fruit experiments were conducted on strawberries. It is only in the last couple of years that we have become aware of irradiation as more research has appeared in print, and the results of that research are quite alarming. According to Dr Donald Louria, chairman of the Department of Preventive Medicine and Community Health at the University of Medicine and Dentistry of New Jersey, nuclear waste used in this process takes many years to break down. He claims that research done to date, used as a basis for allowing the irradiation process, were poorly documented. In these experiments, laboratory animals died for no apparent reason. If cats living on a diet of cooked food deteriorate drastically and become sexually deviant and sterile after three generations (according to Dr F M Pottenger in his book *Pottenger's Cats*), how will irradiated foods affect us after a couple of generations? The effects on one generation has not yet been studied satisfactorily. Dr Louria also states that no irradiation plant is environmentally safe.

Dr Richard Piccioni, a senior staff scientist with Accord Research, claims that chemical changes take place when food is irradiated so that both known and unknown carcinogens and mutagens are formed in irradiated food. He also says that too little research has been done. Dr George Trisch, a cancer research scientist in Buffalo, New York, says that mutagenic and carcinogenic substances are formed during this process and that formaldehyde (a very toxic substance) is formed in carbohydrates. Dr Trisch states that in research done on children and animals, more chromosomes appear in the cell (as seen in tumours), and that carcinogenic substances are formed when unsaturated fats are irradiated. Both fruit and vegetables contain carbohydrates and unsaturated fats, therefore, when fruit and vegetables are irradiated, formaldehyde and carcinogenic substances must be formed, resulting in the degeneration of the health of the consumer.

The most important thing to remember is that food in it's most natural state is best for us. If it is preserved or coloured, had it's flavour 'enhanced' or been irradiated, we come off second best. A diet that excludes foods containing additives and includes a high intake of fresh, raw food is the best diet for both physical, mental and emotional well-being. As a safeguard to your family's health, read the ingredients listed on everything you buy. It will cost you nothing and it will preserve your health.

CHAPTER TEN

Exercise, Fresh Air and Sunshine: Are They Really Necessary?

Three areas that are often neglected when it comes to health and weight loss are exercise, fresh air and sunshine. Yet without ensuring that these three are incorporated in our lives on a daily basis, it would be impossible to achieve and maintain optimum levels of health and weight control. Once again, it is vital to acknowledge the importance of a holistic life-style, in other words a life-style which includes all those things that pertain to health.

LET'S START WITH EXERCISE

There is absolutely no way around it – exercise is necessary. We are designed to exercise, just as birds are designed to fly. We have over 400 muscles in our bodies, and as much as we enjoy our modern, labour-saving devices, those muscles were designed to work! So what should we do – throw away our car keys, vacuum cleaners and washing machines? Well, that would do wonders for the environment, but it is not quite practical in this day and age. What each of us should be doing, is finding an exercise programme that suits us best and which fits comfortably into our life-styles.

What sort of exercise you might ask? Most importantly, you should be doing an aerobic form of exercise. Not necessarily aerobics classes in leotards, but exercising aerobically or 'with air'. In other words, you should try an exercise that requires you to work your lungs and heart at a steady pace, rather than the stop-start variety. Examples of aerobic exercise are brisk walking, running, cycling, swimming and yes, aerobics in a gym.

Of all of these, walking is the most natural form of exercise for man to do, and you are also less likely to suffer from injuries. An added bonus is that you don't need special shoes or clothing, although flat shoes and loose comfortable clothing are ideal. When I suggest walking, I mean brisk walking that gets your lungs going and your heart pumping. To do this you need to swing your arms and stride out with purpose. Almost anyone can walk. Start by walking around your garden, then around the block. If you're nervous, take a friend or your dog along with you.

What if you don't like walking? Well, find something that you do enjoy. There are plenty of people who have some type of exercise machine hidden away in the depths of the garage. Haul it out! Whatever you do, you must enjoy the exercise, you must feel comfortable and you must not overdo it. Start slowly and build up your level of performance and fitness.

If you are not motivated to exercise on your own, then join an exercise group or good gym so that you can be monitored. Mark and I enjoy a combination of walking, running and cycling, whichever takes our mood that day. We particularly enjoy these forms of exercise because we get out into the fresh air. Sundays we like to go for a long, leisurely ride on our bikes with our girls. In between we garden once a week and, believe it or not, we still get stiff! This just goes to show how many of our muscles are under-utilised. We also enjoy a game of tennis when we get an opportunity to play.

Another form of exercise which we enjoy tremendously is rebounding. Jumping on a mini-trampoline or rebounder is an excellent form of aerobic exercise. It is particularly well suited to confined, indoor areas and is good for when it is pouring with rain or if there is not enough time to get out and exercise. You can even do it while you watch the news on television. There is, in fact, no excuse for not exercising in some way or another.

'How much?' you might ask here. Ideally, you should exercise for no less than twenty minutes a day and preferably between thirty minutes to one hour. 'No time,' you might reply. What if I told you all you need is five minutes a day. That's right, all you need is five minutes a day for the first week, and you can build it up slowly to ten minutes a day for the second week. You then continue adding a couple of minutes each week until you've built up to at least twenty minutes a day.

How do you know if you are overdoing it? The best way is to take your pulse. Feel for your heartbeat at the side of your windpipe in your neck, or on the inside of your wrist. You time your heartbeat for fifteen seconds, after fifteen to twenty minutes of exercise. Let's say this figure is twenty-five beats. You multiply this figure by four to find out the beats per minute. For example, 25 x 4 = 100 beats per minute. To find out if you are doing enough work, you subtract your age from 220. Let's say you are forty years old: 220 – 40 = 180. You then multiply that figure by 60% to get your minimum heart rate after 20 minutes of exercising: 180 x 60% = 108 beats per minute. Your heart at age forty should not beat slower than 108 beats per minute after twenty minutes of aerobic exercise. If it is, then you are not working hard enough. To reach your maximum heart rate, multiply 180 by 85%: 180 x 85% = 153 beats per minute. At age forty, after 20 minutes of exercise, your heart should not beat faster than 153 beats per minute. If it is, then you are working too hard.

The important points to remember about exercise is that it should be:

1. Habitual. It should become a habit and one of the best ways to form a new habit is to exercise at the same time of the day for at least twenty-one days. This is the time that it takes to either make or break a habit. Exercise at whatever time of the day is most convenient for you. Mark and I enjoy the mornings the most as it really gets us in the right frame of mind for the rest of the day.

2. Progressive. Exercise should progress, that is it should start slowly and easily and increase steadily. It's often very tempting to rush out and exercise madly for an hour, thinking that you will get fit more quickly. You won't. You will probably just end up very tired and rather disillusioned.

3. Systematic. Your programme should consist of a system of exercises that does three things:

(a) Works your lungs, like running, walking, swimming and all other forms of aerobic exercise.

(b) Stretches your muscles, although it is better to stretch them after you have warmed up. Try touching your toes before a work-out and after; you'll get down a lot further after the work-out because your muscles have warmed up.

(c) Includes resistance work. No, that's not only weightlifting! Gardening can also be resistance work. Good old press-ups are included here too. A work-out in one of the municipal Trim Parks is also good resistance work.

Do consult a sports or exercise specialist or read up about some good resistance and stretching exercises before you start, as these two types of exercise can lead to injury if performed incorrectly. In fact, it's a good idea to have a check-up with your doctor before you embark on any new exercise programme. A good gym will offer you an intensive assessment and will be able to refer you to a doctor if any problems arise.

At this point, you might want to know how the Natural

Way dietary programme propagated in this book affects one's level of activity. Many sports physiologists have now found that the most important nutrient in exercise is not protein, as once thought, but carbohydrates. The mistake is often made of encouraging people to 'carbo-load' on any carbohydrates, including quantities of refined carbohydrates. This practice will ultimately cause a loss of nutrients and a drop in blood sugar levels which, in the long term, will impede your performance and damage your health. (For more on this, see the chapter on how nutrition affects the mind and the emotions.) Mark and I do a bit of running, our furthest distance being thirty-two kilometres. We find that running on an empty stomach is best and all we drink along the way is water. The energy we need to perform comes from what we ate two days before the run. We find that if we combine our food badly the night before, we feel very flat on the day of the run. Similarly, when we eat a refined carbohydrate, especially sweets, our performance level is affected adversely. I also find that if I eat any dairy products before a run, my stomach and kidneys get quite sore while I'm running. We 'carbo-load' on foods like bananas, dates, raisins, potatoes, brown rice and mealies. As for our children, they do extremely well on this programme. Melissa has been awarded her colours for swimming and netball, and we find that when exercising with families who eat the 'normal' way, our children have more endurance. So do we for that matter! I have also found that every single person I know who follows this programme, has experienced a vast increase in energy levels and endurance.

Remember that correct nutrition without exercise is not enough, and that vigorous exercise with a bad diet can be dangerous! Strive for a good balance and whatever you choose to do, get moving and keep moving.

WHAT ABOUT FRESH AIR?

More important than any other requirement in life, is the air we breath. Without air we would be lucky to be alive for longer than five to ten minutes. For this reason, we should try our best to live, dress and carry ourselves in a way that does not affect our breathing adversely.

We should ensure that we have sufficient ventilation in our homes. In my consultations, I have often been surprised by the number of people who sleep with their windows shut at night. Even if you are worried about security, sleep with a top window open at least. I have found that the wider the window is open, the more fresh I feel in the morning. In winter on the Highveld, which can be very cold, Mark and I still sleep with our windows wide open. There is nothing worse than waking up with a thick head after a night of inhaling your own carbon dioxide (which is a waste product). If you have to leave your home unattended during the day, give it a good airing every morning, by flinging open all doors and windows when you get up, and then shut them just before you leave. When you get home in the afternoon, do the same again. If it is cold, dress more warmly or put extra blankets on your bed. If the evening is cool, pull a rug over your legs, rather than shutting a window or switching on a heater. To keep your home fresh and odour-free, good ventilation and plenty of fresh air is the answer.

In order to dress in a manner that does not impede your breathing, you should wear clothes that are loose-fitting. This does not mean that you have to walk around in baggy sacks. Today's fashions allow for loose-fitting, elegant clothes. In fact, you can even wear tailored outfits provided that they are not skin-tight. Tight clothing inhibits air circulation next to your skin and discourages your body from ridding itself of toxins through the skin. This results in your body becomes toxin-laden and you could end up with skin rashes. Clothing made of natural fibres are the best to wear as these fabrics allow your skin to breathe freely. Natural-fibre clothing is not necessarily more expensive; cotton garments are freely available from most clothing outlets at reasonable prices.

Posture is an important factor in obtaining sufficient air. To carry yourself in a manner that encourages correct breathing is to walk upright with your shoulders back and stomach in, just as our mothers have always told us. Not only will your breathing be better, but mentally you'll feel ready to take on the world!

To ensure that you get sufficient air at all times, avoid ill-ventilated, stuffy rooms (you don't want to breathe in someone else's waste products), wear comfortable garments made of natural fabrics, and walk tall.

ADD A LITTLE SUNSHINE

Without sunshine it would not be possible to be healthy; even plants die when they are not exposed to sunlight for some time. Yet the sun has been much maligned with the result that many people avoid it at all costs to the detriment of their health.

One wonders whether this fear of sunshine is not propagated by companies wanting to push their unnatural chemical preparations, such as block-outs, sun screens and moisturisers. There have been some reports recently which suggest that block-outs could in fact cause cancer. This makes sense as the block-out preparations are foreign chemicals which are applied to the skin. I know that in the past when I tried applying these preparations to my own skin, they caused a burning sensation and often resulted in a bit of a rash, even though I tried various respected brands.

The important thing to remember is that the skin is an organ of elimination. If it is continually called upon to eliminate the carcinogenic toxins which we have taken in with our food, then this must be detrimental to the skin. This is especially true of areas exposed to the sun, as the sun speeds up elimination thereby increasing the amount of toxin release through that section of the skin. This accelerated process of elimination is the more likely cause of skin cancer.

But, let's get back to the crux of the issue. Is the sun good or bad for you? The sun is essential for your health and well-being but excessive exposure can be harmful. Your body needs exposure to sunlight so that it can synthesize vitamin D. This in turn helps your body to assimilate or utilise calcium. This could well be another reason why so many more women than men develop osteoporosis or brittle bones, as they tend to stay out of the sun far more than men, due to the so-called 'ageing' effects of the sun. Sunlight also affects the number of red cells and haemoglobin in the blood. Too little sunlight results in the serum, or watery portion of the blood, increasing with a proportionate decrease in the fibrin (blood protein) and red blood cells, thus causing anaemia.

I recall a forty-year-old professional medical woman coming to see me. She had been taking iron tablets and had been eating liver for a couple of years, in vast quantities, but to no avail. She remained anaemic and her level of health continued to deteriorate. After questioning her about her habits, I found that she worked from 7.00 a.m. to 8.00 p.m. every day, often including Saturdays and Sundays. She said that she never had the time to go outside or to sit in the sun. Her whole body had a pale, flabby look about it and her skin had an uneven quality. After discontinuing the iron tablets (which were causing her to be constipated) and the liver (which she hated), I then corrected her diet and included twenty minutes of sunbathing a day in her programme. Within a month her iron levels were up, dramatically, and the overall improvement of her health was significant, as was the quality of her skin.

In addition to its other properties, the sun also helps to build a better quality flesh, it enables us to assimilate food more efficiently, it stimulates glandular or endocrine activity, it helps with irregularities of ovulation, difficulties in puberty, impotence, acne, psoriasis and nervous disorders, and it also accelerates hair growth and helps to strengthen the eyes.

But as much good as the sun does, it is important not to go out in its peak period between about 11.30 a.m. or 12 noon until about 2.30 p.m. If you don't stay out of the sun at this time of the day, then you most certainly will damage your skin, as its heat is at its most intense. Your body with its innate intelligence, has the built-in ability to tell you that it has had enough sun. This happens when you begin to feel hot, sticky and uncomfortable. Don't go leaping into a pool to cool down and then get back into the sun as you will certainly be overdoing it. Twenty minutes to one hour in the sun on a daily basis is more than enough to maintain good health without doing any damage.

As far as oils and lotions are concerned, avoid them! They only clog up the pores and prevent the sebaceous or oil glands from functioning correctly, resulting in the skin drying out in the long term. Premature ageing and poor texture are sure to result.

Remember that without regular exercise, a continual supply of fresh air and a daily dose of sunshine, you cannot even begin to achieve or maintain the vibrant health that is your right.

CHAPTER ELEVEN

How to Really
Treat Your Skin

Much has been written about the skin and yet there is so much confusion. Let's start with the basics. Why do we have a skin?

The skin is an organ of sensitivity, which enables us to feel various sensations. When you touch something hot your immediate reaction is to withdraw your finger from the heat source. The same thing happens when you go into the sun. After about half an hour you feel very hot and uncomfortable. This is because your skin is doing its job as an organ of sensitivity and is sending out warning signals to prevent damage. Once again, listen to your body, especially when it comes to your skin and the sun, unless you enjoy looking like a prune.

The skin is also an organ of elimination, which simply means that it provides the body with a mechanism to cleanse itself. A simple skin rash is often nothing more than an indication that the body is eliminating something foreign or toxic and this process results in an inflammation of the skin. I find, for example, that I get hives or urticaria (a type of skin rash) from a particular additive that is used in some chocolates. My skin becomes extremely inflamed when this substance is excreted through it. More often than not, a rash or similar skin condition is caused by incorrect eating. By rectifying this, most skin conditions clear. Interestingly enough, although the severe dermatitis that I suffered from on my hands cleared up totally within four days of combining my food correctly, it would reappear when I went back to poor eating habits. This condition could have many causes such as the alcohol, acetic acid, ammonia or even histamines which are formed when food ferments in the stomach due to incorrect combinations. These toxic substances are then excreted through the skin. This generally affects only those people with so-called sensitive skins. The body uses one of the other excretory organs (lungs, bowels or bladder) in those people not susceptible to skin problems.

The skin is also an organ of nutrition in that it synthesizes vitamin D from the sun. Vitamin D is an important nutrient which plays a role in maintaining calcium levels and phosphorous metabolism in the body. Vitamin D is also thought to play a role in iron assimilation.

The skin is also an organ of protection. It acts as a shield and protects the body against bacterial and other infection.

Now, how should you really treat your skin? The most important thing is to eat correctly. Never before has the old adage, 'you are what you eat', been more true than when it is applied to the skin. Many people I have dealt with have benefited their skins tremendously by correcting their eating habits. I was diagnosed as having a 'dry, sensitive' skin. I cannot begin to record all the expensive, imported skin preparations that I so naïvely smeared onto my face. The result? I was broke and I still had a 'dry, sensitive skin'. In this disillusioned state I returned to a good old bar of pH balanced soap, at a price, and still no improvement. The most dramatic change came about when I started eating a predominantly raw diet.

I also realised that if soap strips off the acid mantle (the skin's natural acidity) from the face then surely the rest of the skin must react in the same way. I investigated body brushing as an alternative to soap and for many years now

I have used no soap on any part of my body. My skin is softer and cleaner than it has been in years! As soap is alkaline, it counteracts the natural acidity of the skin which has a pH level of about 5.5. This results in an alkaline environment, ideal for the proliferation of bacteria. As bacteria breed far quicker in an alkaline environment, sores and scratches will become septic more easily if you are using soap. Soap also removes natural oils from the surface of the skin, leaving it dry and taut. Washing with soap does not remove surface dead skin cells, resulting in that flaky, dry look. Body brushing, with a loofah or natural bristle brush – not nylon, which will damage your skin – on the other hand, keeps both the pH balance and the natural oils intact, yet removes the dead skin cells from the surface.

Since I stopped using soap, I have not needed any moisturiser, blockout, sunscreen or hand and body lotion, yet my skin is now in peak condition. No more burning cheeks, dry legs and hands or cracked heels for me! Ask yourself, does it make sense to remove your natural oils and then to replace them with an artificial chemical or even so-called natural, herbal mixture?

It is only because of years and years of eating the foods that our systems were not designed to consume, that our skins start to play up and give trouble. Add to that excessive exposure to very strong sunlight and artificial skin preparations, and you have the answer to premature ageing of the skin.

If you have never brushed your body, now is the time to start! Bristle brushing can be done either on dry skin before you bath, as the Europeans suggest, or in the bath or shower as Mark prefers. I suggest you brush you body once a day only, preferably in the morning as this is when there are the most dead skin cells on the surface of your skin. During the night while you sleep, your skin replaces old cells at two-and-a-half times the rate it normally does. (Remember the body cycles and how your body repairs more while you sleep.) I brush my face with a soft bristle brush (a shaving brush can be used although I prefer something a bit firmer). Remember to be gentle with the skin on your face. I do this in the mornings only. At night I use a clean cotton face-cloth with warm water. If I wear make-up, I remove it with water. I tend to stick to the water soluble products not tested on animals.

A word of warning is necessary. It did take about a year to wean myself off all creams and for my own skin to achieve an optimum balance by producing just enough oil to prevent either oiliness or dryness. I achieved this by applying creams less and less frequently; from once a day, to once every two days, until I used creams only on days that my skin was a bit too dry. Eventually I found that I could go without any skin care products at all.

If you are using a skin care range, use a local one designed for local skins and one which contains no artificial colourants and preservatives or animal products. Also support one that does no testing on animals and use a pH balanced cleanser on the rest of your body.

Smoking cigarettes probably does more damage to the skin than any other bad habit. Smoking starves the skin of many nutrients, resulting in a grey, slack appearance. Without fail, I can pin-point the smokers just by the tone and colour of their skins. Another habit that affects the skin adversely is the consumption of alcohol. The regular tipplers can be spotted by the tiny blood capillaries under the skin which tend to burst, resulting in a tell-tale blotchy, uneven tone. Remember that by combining your food badly, alcohol is formed. It then gets into the blood-stream and is transported throughout the body, including the skin.

Exercise is also of great benefit to the skin as it gets the heart pumping faster. This, in turn, gets more nutrients speedily to the skin and achieves that 'healthy glow'. Fresh air and sunshine also have a vital role to play. (I find that being in an air-conditioned or heated room dries the skin out terribly.)

So you don't have to spend a fortune on your skin after all. With the correct diet and sensible habits including regular exercise, fresh air and sunshine you can have a healthy, glowing skin for life.

CHAPTER TWELVE

Water: How Much, How Often?

Water is one of the most life-giving substances available to us. Without it, we would die within a few days. No life can exist without water – there would be no animals and no plants in the absence of this precious liquid.

Our bodies are made up of approximately sixty per cent water. It makes sense therefore, that our diet should contain at least the same percentage of water. By consuming a diet high in fresh fruit and vegetables, you would automatically be meeting this basic requirement. We obtain our water not only from food and fluids, but also from internal oxidation reactions. The hydrogen content of the food we eat combines with the oxygen which we breathe – and the reaction of two hydrogen molecules combining with one molecule of oxygen, forms water (H_2O).

Water has many vital roles. It is needed for removal of waste through kidney and bowels, lungs and skin. It regulates our body temperature. It is needed for the digestion process and for enzyme manufacturing. It lubricates our joints, and it is also needed for the correct functioning of the glandular system. The hypothalamus situated below the brain regulates the conservation, replenishment and elimination of water. These processes can be affected by the types of water we drink since inorganic mineral deposits can impair the functioning of the hypothalamus, and can easily damage the thyroid, adrenal and pituitary glands.

About three quarters of the body fluid is stored within the cells, and without water, they would literally shrivel up and die. Blood plasma, which transports mineral salts, carbohydrates, proteins, gases, enzymes, fats and hormones, is approximately ninety-two per cent water. All the nutrients that we take into our bodies are ultimately broken down to become water soluble. In other words, they are able to dissolve in water. The whole aim of the digestive process is to break food down so that it dissolves easily in water. In this way the nutrients can be transported throughout the system by the blood. Drinking during a meal does not facilitate this process. It tends to dilute the digestive enzymes in the stomach so that the food is then not easily broken down. This can also result in fermentation, even though the meal might be properly combined. It is best to drink half an hour before the meal, or one to two hours after the meal.

There are no set rules for how much water should be consumed. The higher the water content of your foods, the less additional water you will need, but the lower the water content, the more water you will need to drink. On hot days, or on days when you exercise more, you will need to drink more water than on other days. You will also find that you need more water when there are condiments in your food. The reason for this is that condiments are foreign or toxic to the cells and need to be suspended in a diluted solution so as not to harm the tissues. When you start listening to your body, you will not only be able to feel how it responds to a highly spiced or salted meal, but you will be able to understand why it reacts that way. This is one of the most important reasons for keeping your meals simple.

On the Natural Way programme you will find that the eight glasses of water per day that we have always been told to drink, is far too much. This is because the foods that you will be eating have a high water content. There are no hard and fast rules about how much water you need – your body will 'tell' you with a natural thirst. Listening to your body is most important here. If you are thirsty, drink water, not tea or coffee or soft drinks. Drinking water beyond your thirst for the sake of consuming eight glasses of water a day just puts tremendous unnecessary strain on your kidneys.

What kind of water is best? Certainly not the water that comes from our taps in South Africa. According to two Water Engineers P Polasch and C C Margeot, South Africa's level of water purification is unsatisfactory. There are numerous reasons for this, including absence of research into advance water purification technology, lack of specialised staff, and lack of proper control and monitoring. To quote from their paper entitled 'Shortcomings in water purification practices in South Africa':

> South Africa is probably the only country among the industrialised nations which does not have a stringent standard for drinking water ... drinking water must not contain such organisms or such concentrations of substances which after long-term ingestion could have a detrimental effect on the health of man.

They proceed to explain how low our standards are, for example, The European Environmental Committee limit on chlorides is 25 milligrams per litre, the World Health Organisation's is 200 mg/l, but the South African Bureau of Standards 1984 limit is 600 mg/l. Polasch and Margeot claim that cadmium and mercury are cumulative poisons which affect the liver. Cadmium causes anaemia, decalcification of bones and liver diseases, while mercury attacks the central nervous system. Both substances are present in our drinking water. The EEC cadmium limit is 0,005 mg/l and it sets its mercury limit at 0,001 mg/l. The SABS sets its limit on cadmium at 0,02 mg/l (four times as much as the EEC's) and on mercury at 0,01 mg/l (ten times as much). The following table makes further comparisons of the toxic minerals in our water:

	(SABS) 1971	(SABS) 1984	EEC
Arsenic	0,05	0,3	0,05
Manganese	0,04	1,0	0,05
Hexavalent Chromium	0,05	No Limit	0,05
Cyanide	0,2	0,3	0,05
Phenolic Compounds	0,002	0,01	0,0005
Sulphates	400	600	250

Polasch and Margeot go on to highlight further inadequacies in our water purification system:

- South Africa has no set level for carcinogenic (cancer inducing) substances in its water.
- There is no set limit for the aluminium content. They point out that aluminium affects the mental processes of man adversely. By comparison the EEC standard is 0,05 mg/l.
- Drinking water should be odourless, tasteless (but palatable) and colourless. Yet the SABS's 1984 limit for colour does not stipulate the maximum allowable level. The SABS level is 20 mg/l as opposed to the EEC limit, which is 1 mg/l.
- Many of the drinking waters in South Africa have a greenish tint due to so-called vegetation colour. These can result in the formation of toxic substances in the human body. Yet the health authorities have no objection to this green tint.
- While the rest of the world is attempting to improve the quality of drinking water, South Africa has adopted the opposite approach as is demonstrated in the table where the 1971 standards are higher than those of 1984.

- The SABS only addresses some 27 parameters of water quality as opposed to the EEC's 70 parameters.
- They close this section of their paper saying, 'It transpires from the foregoing that the SABS 241/84 does not reflect modern health requirements and also does not take into consideration the fact of continuously deteriorating quality of water in our drinking water sources'. This news is indeed alarming!

A point not covered fully in this document is the effect of chlorinated water. (Bear in mind that world-wide, much of the drinking water is chlorinated.) Chlorine has been found to contribute to arteriosclerosis (hardening of the arteries), asthma attacks, nausea and disorientation. In addition, chlorine is a powerful irritant which also destroys vitamin E. This vitamin is a natural antioxidant which helps to prevent cancer.

As for fluoride, if it really did prevent tooth decay, there would be a marked decrease in dental decay as this substance is also present in our water. Fluoride has been found to stimulate bone formation, but the bone is poorly mineralised and brittle. Fluoride is also toxic to the rest of the body. Dr Leo Spiro, who was awarded a degree in recognition of his research on fluoridation by the London University, says that fluoride damages brain and nerve cells, is harmful to reproductive organs, affects the thyroid gland, damages the liver, and creates a high incidence of bone fracture. He adds that, 'We cannot prophecy what would happen to the organs of the body if it were subjected to constant doses of fluoride for a lifetime'. Fluoride is one of those industrial waste products that someone decided would be of benefit, without having done any long-term tests on the effect it would have on the human body.

There is not much you can do at the point of purification, but at least you can do something about the quality of the water in your own home. You can filter your water quite easily by using any of the variety of filter jugs or pottery filters currently available. For the most part they are practical and easy to use, and remove chlorine and organic contaminants from the water. As there are so many domestic water purification systems on the market, I suggest that you look for an established brand, backed by solid research, which will be able to supply you with replacement filters or cartridges for years to come. If you can afford it, a reverse osmosis purifier is best, but it does waste a lot of water. Ultimately, all drinking water should be filtered, and so too should any water that you use for cooking.

A question I am often asked is, 'What about mineral water?' Although bottled water is rich in minerals, unfortunately these minerals are not present in a form that our bodies are able to use easily. Unlike the minerals in fresh fruits and vegetables, those in mineral water are easily deposited in our joints, muscles and tissues, where they can cause stiffness, gall or kidney stones, premature ageing of the skin and even cataracts. Do not be alarmed. This does not mean that you should never touch mineral water – it is probably the best type of drink you could have in a social situation. Merely limit your intake. I would say that one glass a day should be the maximum that you consume. If you have a choice, go for the non-carbonated variety, as the bubbles in sparkling mineral water are formed by carbon dioxide, a waste product which the body tries to eliminate. It doesn't make sense to force carbon dioxide into the body when it has gone to so much trouble to get rid of it in the first place.

Before you drown in all this detail, remember that you should listen to your body when it comes to water. When thirsty, drink clean filtered water. A diet high in fresh raw fruit and vegetables is able to supply a great deal of the water your body needs. Remember that fruit, our ideal food, contains as much as eighty to ninety per cent pure water. If you need to drink socially, go for natural, unsweetened, preservative-free fruit juices or mineral waters. Try to leave out the fizz if you can. But even with the bubbles, these choices are still better than any of the artificial cooldrinks on the market. (Try not to drink more than one glass of commercial fruit juice in a day. They are heated to kill bacteria and in the process become quite acidic to the body. A number of the nutrients are also destroyed by this process.) Pure water always comes out tops. A glass of water with a slice of lemon not only tastes good, but looks fashionable too. Cheers!

CHAPTER THIRTEEN

Fasting: The Way to Supreme Health

No! Fasting is not confined to religious fanatics, it just happens to be the fastest way to supreme health, well-being and optimum weight levels.

During a fast, the body redirects the energy it would otherwise use for digesting meals and other daily activities, to any problem area in the body. In other words, the body is given an opportunity to focus on cleansing and healing. Weight loss is also achieved more quickly on a fast as the body burns any excess fat deposits for fuelling its normal functions. (The average weight loss is from half to one kilogram per day.)

People often refer to abstaining from solid foods but drinking juice as a 'juice fast'. This is, in fact, not a fast at all but a diet. A juice diet to be exact. There is only one kind of fast and that is a total abstinence from nourishment of any kind. Even taking in honey or grapefruit juice does not make it a true fast.

True fasting thus means eating nothing at all, drinking only pure water, and resting both physically and mentally. Rest is what a fast is all about. A true fast allows the body and mind to rest completely and to redirect energy towards healing and correcting any problems that may exist. Complete rest is vitally important when fasting as it restores the body physically, emotionally and mentally. The ideal setting should be a quiet place away from the family, work, television, radio and the general hustle and bustle of everyday life. The last thing you need on a fast is stress of any description. The mind and body must be in a state of repose.

The benefits of fasting are tremendous. Your general health improves, your skin and eyes glow and you feel as if you've had a total 'overhaul' or body-lift. A properly supervised fast followed by a correct eating programme, is the best and quickest way to glowing health.

A word of caution is needed here. Fasting for more than two to three days should not be embarked on without the guidance of a health counsellor or someone who has both studied and undergone a fast themselves. Do not rush into a fast. It is essential that you are adequately prepared for the fast and properly supervised while fasting. If you are pregnant, lactating or on any medication you should be extremely cautious. Fasting is not recommended under these circumstances. If you plan to fast even with the aid of a counsellor, read as much as you can on the subject before you begin. Ideally, you should eat only raw foods for as many days before and after as you would be on the fast. In other words, if you are planning a two-day fast, stick to raw foods for two days before you begin, and continue with raw foods for two days after. You don't just start fasting because you have over-indulged and want to punish yourself. A fast must be planned carefully.

Fasting employed correctly, can result in the body performing miracles. I have seen this not only in myself, but in many other people as well. Take the case of Ingrid, aged twenty-one. Ingrid was diagnosed as having a cyst close to her anus and was told that her only option was surgery. Ingrid chose instead to fast. She started by eating fruit only for a week before the fast (this was to ensure that there was no fermenting, old food in her digestive tract other than fruit.) She then embarked on a true fast. By the fifth day of the fast, Ingrid reported that her urine and body odour smelt very strongly of Roaccutane. This is a so-called 'miracle-drug' that was prescribed for her skin a year previously at an exorbitant cost for a six-month treatment. Ingrid was warned at the time that she should not fall pregnant for at least a year, as the drug could damage the foetus. (Latest research indicates that this period should be five years.) All that the drug seemed to achieve was to dehydrate her nasal passages, eyes and skin terribly. Ingrid said that her urine continued to have this odour for a couple more days and that by the eighth day of the fast, the cyst had broken down completely. She then broke her fast by drinking fresh fruit juice, and continued to eat fruit and raw vegetables, until she gradually introduced cooked vegetables and carbohydrates. Now, six months later, the cyst has not reappeared.

Sandy on the other hand, aged thirty-eight, had numerous complaints. She suffered from candida (a type of yeast infection) which resulted in severe digestive problems. Her stomach bloated virtually every time she ate something. (Candida usually results from use of antibiotics, the contraceptive pill and a diet that is high in processed and refined foods.) Even after changing her diet to the Natural Way programme, Sandy still battled with the candida, although there was an improvement in her general health. Encouraged by her doctor, Sandy came to me for a fasting programme. She was able to take time off work and managed to fast, very comfortably I might add, for sixteen days. At this stage Sandy felt that she would like to continue her fast, but she needed to get back to work. Sandy had a medical check-up, including blood tests, before and after the fast. Before the fast, her doctor said that her liver was not functioning propery, that she could not assimilate or absorb potassium effectively, and that she had the previously mentioned candida problem. After the fast her potassium levels were in the top of the range (from 3.5 m/mol to 4.8 m/mol), her liver was functioning one hundred per cent and the candida problem had cleared up.

Fasting, as can be seen from these case studies, is to be taken seriously and should not be undertaken on a whim. Although fasting for one day a week or once a month is easily achieved and gives the digestive tract a good rest, anything longer should be supervised by an experienced consultant. The duration of your fast depends on your general state of health, your fat reserves and on whoever is supervising you. There have been cases where severely obese people have fasted for up to three months, and then there are frequently cases where individuals should not fast for more than a day or two at most.

Fasting for a day or two before changing your diet is also a good way to kick-start you into a correct eating programme. This way you make a clean start and somehow after a fast, all that fresh raw food tastes so good. It is also one of the quickest ways I know to stop smoking. I have yet to discover anyone who can fast and still smoke at the same time. Your body is also able to rid itself of the toxins from smoking far more quickly on a fast, and once the fast is broken there is no craving or hankering after the taste of tobacco.

I am deliberately not going into too much detail on fasting in this chapter, as I merely wish to point you in the right direction and ensure that you find a person who is experienced in fasting to help you. (Fasting is a subject that requires a book of its own!) In the last few years, I have been able to train many people in the principles of fasting, and if you write to me, I could let you have the name of a supervisor closest to you. One of the main reasons that you should find someone to monitor your fast is that the symptoms of detoxification which usually accompany a fast, can be unpleasant. These symptoms could include headaches, migraines, dizziness, nausea, dry mouth, muscle cramps, sores in the mouth, and a strong, unpleasant body odour. These symptoms are unpleasant and can be very frightening if you do not know what to expect. What happens when you fast is that toxins and waste products begin to pour from the system at a very rapid rate. In fact, depending on your previous life-style, the symptoms are not dissimilar to those of drug withdrawal at times. These symptoms may also be experienced in a milder form when you change your diet to a more healthy one such as the Natural Way programme.

To recap, fasting is a wonderfully quick and efficient way to regain health, lose weight and give your body a rest. However, unpleasant symptoms may be experienced and these can be frightening if you are not being supervised or have not prepared yourself beforehand by reading as much as possible on the subject. It is also vital to start and break a fast correctly and only a trained supervisor can help you with this.

CHAPTER FOURTEEN

Weight Loss and Weight Gain: The Secret

In my experience, people who have a weight problem usually overeat (especially on fats) and do not get enough exercise.

There are other factors involved, such as a metabolism ruined by going on too many fad or 'crash' diets. These only encourage your body to store fuel more effectively and efficiently so as to be ready for the next time you starve yourself.

Another reason often given for a weight problem is hormonal imbalance or a glandular problem. This is often used as an excuse for bad living habits. Many people who have this 'problem' are often extremely undisciplined in their eating habits and frequently eat late at night. If a glandular problem truly exists (blood tests would confirm this), then this condition can be sorted out in the long term by eating correctly. For example, refined sugar in the diet can affect the blood sugar level, and this in turn can affect the function of the pituitary gland, the adrenal glands and the thyroid gland. The glandular function then affects the hormonal levels in the body and this can influence the rate of weight loss or gain. Just by eliminating refined sugar from the diet, these glands could return to normal function. Vinegar is another substance which can affect the thyroid gland. When an organ or gland is continually stimulated artificially (as in this case) its activity can become depressed. In other words, from continual stimulation, the thyroid gland can slow down and not function as efficiently as it should. This could result in a sluggish metabolism and difficulty in losing weight. Remember that vinegar is a by-product of fermentation in the stomach, yet another reason to combine your food properly. Mustard oil, found in garlic and onion, can also affect the thyroid gland. Mustard oil can, through a series of events, suppress the production of the hormone thyroxin, which is the hormone that regulates the rate at which we burn fuel. By cutting these substances out of the diet those organs and glands affected will eventually function correctly. I have found that this can take from two months to two years, or longer. (A supervised fast regulates these glands very quickly – see the chapter on fasting.)

Another reason for a persistent weight problem could be that you are on some type of medication – anything from the pill to thyroid drugs, or even plain old headache tablets or laxatives could be the culprit. Any drug can play havoc with your body and I suggest that with the help of a good doctor, you wean yourself off all medication. To achieve this, you would start by taking a smaller dose, that is if you were taking 10 mg of medication, you would start by reducing your intake to 5 mg. You would then progress to taking it every second day, then every third day, and so on until you were able to limit your intake to once a week. Finally you will be able to stop altogether. *It is vital that you consult a doctor before attempting to wean yourself off any medication.*

Often it is difficult to know where to start in order to achieve a slimmer, healthier body. Many people have asked me for a diet sheet as a guide to how much to eat and how often. I have always been reluctant to do this as the Natural Way programme is not so much a diet as a life-style and you must learn to listen to your body and its own particular needs. But I have since come to realise that for many dieters who have followed a regime that requires everything to be weighed and measured, to now change over to a life-style that allows them to eat as much as they like, is like giving an alcoholic the key to a bottle-store. As a result, I've put together various flexible programmes which make the transition easier. What you have to do is decide which programme suits you best. That way you are making the final decision and are not left feeling totally restricted.

Before you start, remember that this is a life-style, not a religion! You can adapt your meals within the Natural Way principles. There will be times when you will cheat or fail to stick to the programme. Do not become disheartened, instead follow the guide-lines in this chapter to help you get over these times and prevent them from recurring too often. Take note – I said 'too often' not 'ever again'. Don't be unrealistic, we live in a world filled with an endless variety of junk food that is packaged, designed and promoted in such a way to get us drooling. We have restaurants and fast-food outlets on every corner, just begging us to come in and celebrate something. But do not despair. You will be able to resist temptation if you stick to a few simple basics:

1. Do your best to combine your food correctly. If you can't, skipping the next meal often does wonders to sort out the mess in your stomach. But don't do this too often as you will merely be taking one step forward and two back. If you are still hungry after a badly-combined meal, then stick to neutral salads and vegetables (see Food Combining Chart at the back of the book).

2. Do not feel guilty if you break the rules. You'll be paying enough of a price physically so don't make it worse by punishing yourself mentally as well. Guilt can often cause you to go on a rebellious binge, which will cause even more damage both mentally and physically.

3. Do not stock 'no-no's' anywhere in your home. If ice-cream, cakes, biscuits and chocolates are bad for you, they are equally bad for your family. It is not a sign of good house-keeping to always have a tub of ice-cream in the deepfreeze or a stock of biscuits in a tin. It is simply a bad habit. No matter how strong-willed you think you are, you will want to eat these snacks just because they are there.

4. Do at all times keep as large a variety of the good things in stock and let them be on display. You know what it's like when all that's in the house is a couple of bananas and one or two apples – boring, boring, boring. Who would possibly feel like fruit? But imagine a couple of strategically placed bowls or baskets filled to overflowing with nectarines, pineapples, mangoes, minneolas, kiwi fruit, naartjies, grapes, plums and peaches, and perhaps even a bowl or two of dates, raisins or nuts. Who could possibly resist?

5. Remember that presentation is almost as important as taste. If food doesn't look good, you don't feel like eating it. Concentrate on making the good food look even better. With very little effort a salad can look far more enticing than a jam doughnut.

Here follow three basic guide-lines, based on the Natural Way programme, to help you establish good health-giving eating habits. What you must do, is decide which of the three you feel most comfortable with and which one enables you to maintain your weight at the right level.

OPTION 1

Wake-up
Glass of one of the following: water, hot water and fresh lemon, or freshly-squeezed fruit juice.

Breakfast

Half a large pawpaw filled with a sliced banana and 5 chopped dates. Or 1 banana, 1 apple and 1 pear, diced together and sprinkled with 100 ml raisins or dried, unbleached sultanas. Or any three fruits from the sweet and sub-acid columns (see chart at the back of the book) with 100 ml of dates or raisins or sultanas.

Mid-morning (between 10 a.m. and noon)

Try any one of the following options:

1 whole pineapple
2 oranges
3 naartjies
2 mangoes
5 kiwi fruit
2 apples
3 – 4 peaches
1 large bunch of grapes
8 litchis
8 strawberries
6 apricots
2 pears
as much watermelon or other melon as you like

Mid-morning and breakfast may be swapped, just make sure you are getting a good variety of fruit. No tea or coffee should be drunk during the morning. (The caffeine will affect your kidneys, and you will end up retaining water.) Drink only water, either hot or cold. Fresh fruit juice may also be drunk and then only if you are thirsty. Ensure that you leave at least one hour between lunch and the last fruit you eat. This will prevent the fermentation of the fruit with the other foods in your stomach.

Lunch

Make a very large salad with any of the following ingredients – lettuce, tomato, celery, red pepper, carrot, spinach, sprouts, cabbage, broccoli, cauliflower, grated butternut, baby marrows, mushrooms, green beans, or any other raw vegetable. Half an avocado may be added to this or used in the following dressing: blend together half an avocado, a little celery, a strip of red pepper, herbal salt and a tomato. Add some water if it is too thick. This salad may be eaten on its own or, if you are very hungry, with one of the following:

1 large baked potato
2 mealies (corn on the cob)
1 medium bowl of brown rice
2 slices home-made wholewheat bread
3 rye biscuits
4 wholewheat biscuits
1 wholewheat pita bread

Mid-afternoon (4.00 p.m. to 5.00 p.m.)

A portion of any fruit – one type of fruit such as an apple or an orange.

Supper

Supper must be started with a large, fresh salad followed with as many steamed vegetables as you like. You may add any of the starches mentioned for lunch if all you had then was the salad. Alternatively, you may like to add half a cup of unsalted unroasted nuts, or a portion of oven-grilled fish or chicken. For a more tasty option, place the chicken or fish in a casserole dish with mushrooms, celery, red pepper or any vegetable of your choice, adding herbal salt and a selection of herbs.

Lunch and supper may be swapped but remember, do not have either starch or protein more than once a day. In other words, if you have a potato for lunch, you should not have rice for supper, and if you had nuts for lunch you should not have fish for supper. Try not to eat after 8.00 p.m. but if you need to snack after supper, any raw vegetable is suitable.

OPTION 2

This is the way my family eats. It is a lot easier than Option 1, not only in preparation but also when it comes to listening to your body.

Wake-up

A glass of water (preferably filtered).

Breakfast

A glass of freshly-squeezed juice, usually orange as it is the most convenient to extract. In my family, most of us are usually not particularly hungry until about 10.00 a.m. and since we now listen to our bodies, we don't eat much until then. We find it convenient to eat nuts at breakfast-time. We tend to stick to almonds as they are very high in protein and calcium, and relatively low in fat, and eat ¼ to ½ cup each with our acid fruit.

Mid-morning

Two to five pieces of any fruit (properly combined). Most often we will eat just one type of fruit at a time such as 2 to 3 oranges or apples, or just a large bunch of grapes, or 3 to 4 mangoes. On the days where we eat nuts for breakfast, we are not particularly hungry during the morning. It is best to stick to acid or sub-acid fruits for at least 4 hours after a nut meal.

Lunch

We then get hungry again between noon and 2.00 p.m. and eat two bananas and a handful of dates or raisins, for example.

We might have a pineapple or half a pawpaw or whatever is in season and delicious.

Mid-afternoon

At about 3.00 to 5.00 p.m. we might feel peckish and then have a piece of fruit.

Supper

Occasionally this is also fruit, especially in summer when there aren't enough hours in the day to eat all the delicious fruits available. Most often though, we'll start with a large salad consisting of lettuce, tomato, carrots, red pepper, celery, avocado and occasionally, some olives (in brine). Some evenings we make a complete meal of this and others we might have whole baked butternut, steamed broccoli, baked or steamed potatoes, bowls of steaming brown rice, steamed green mealies, a mixed vegetable casserole or a soup. We do have a bit of butter on our cooked food, although I do find that if I'm eating avocado, I do not need the butter. I find olive oil far more palatable than butter, and as it is cold-pressed, unsaturated and cholesterol-free, it is a far healthier choice (it is less fattening too!). If avocado is not freely available (late December to February), we might have a meal of just salad and half a cup of nuts each. Remember that if you are a vegetarian, 100 g of nuts or seeds should be included in your diet at least three times a week.

OPTION 3

This is a cleansing diet and although it is very healthy and efficient in helping you to reach your ideal weight, it is quite difficult to maintain for more than a couple of weeks at a time due to the fact that it is a totally raw-food diet. I would encourage everyone, young, old, fat, thin, sick or healthy to try this at least once a year for a two-week period.

Your day is very similar to that outlined in Option 2 in that you eat fruit all day, whenever you feel hungry. Supper could either be more fruit, or alternatively a large salad with half a cup of unsalted, unroasted nuts, or an avocado. The salad with nuts or avocado should be eaten at least 3 to 4 times a week, but you will find it easier to stick to this programme if you have 50g of nuts or seeds a day. If you are not wanting to lose weight on this raw-food regime, then make sure to eat more avocados, dates and raisins, as well as trying to eat at least two bananas a day.

With all the programmes outlined in this chapter, the most important thing of all is to listen to your body, not to your taste-buds, and to remember that this can take a couple of months to achieve. Also, do not overeat! I cannot reiterate this often enough. Eat slowly, chew carefully and keep it simple. The simpler the meal, the least done to and added to the food, the better. Simple meals are more often far more attractive and tasty than complicated ones, and a great deal more healthy too!

You may find it difficult to stick to your newly chosen eating programme and the sudden introduction of regular exercise into your life-style may cause some discomfort. Refer to the nine points listed below from time to time to help you keep on track.

CHECK-LIST FOR WEIGHT-LOSS

1. Am I exercising aerobically at least five times per week for a minimum period of 30 minutes (walking briskly, swimming, running or cycling)? Exercises such as stretching, tennis, gardening and other stop-start activities, should not be counted in this 30 minute period, but should be regarded as additional exercise. Remember to start slowly and to build up your time gradually – start with five minutes per day, then build up to ten minutes and then 15 minutes until you eventually reach 30 minutes per day. Regular daily exercise, even for only a few minutes, is preferable to starting with 30 minutes of exercise three times a week.

2. Am I off all possible medication? If not, remember to work towards this with the help of a good doctor, one who knows that all drugs are a strain on the body.

3. Am I obeying the most basic rules of the Natural Way programme? These are:
– Fruit in the morning
– A salad with each meal
– Correctly combined meals
– Preferably no red meat, dairy products, tea or coffee
– No additives in any foods
– Minimal amounts of animal fats such as butter and cream
– Eating in moderation, and only when hungry
– Not eating after 8.00 p.m.
– Removing all refined sugar and carbohydrates

4. Am I doing something to renew my mind? For example, read some motivational material on a regular basis. Any bookshop will be able to help you find some stimulating reading matter. The Bible is also very uplifting.

5. Am I developing interests that do not focus on myself or my weight? Go to art lessons, help out at your local school or church, join a help organization such as Childline or Lifeline. I've found that people who have a real emotional problem with food are usually too busy thinking about themselves, their bodies and what goes into them! By doing something that involves helping other people or by learning something new, you take the focus off yourself, and suddenly what you put into your mouth is not of such obsessive interest any more. I remember doing the Dale Carnegie course in 1983. It was a turning-point in my life. Mark and I did the course on Human Relations and Public Speaking together.

By doing the course, I learnt to accept myself, and not to be so critical and judgemental of myself and others. I became more tolerant as a result and stopped feeling guilty about not being Miss Perfect. I started focusing on small successes instead of what I had perceived as huge failures. I think women in particular are too obsessed with an unrealistic image of perfection that we strive towards, and then suffer from tremendous guilt because we haven't attained our impossible goal. Relax and be positive about yourself for a change. Learn to love yourself.

6. Have I identified any trigger events which cause me to eat badly? A trigger event could be an emotion such as happiness, sadness, anger or frustration which makes you want to eat everything in sight. Once you have identified it, you will be able to do something about it when the urge to indulge crops up.

7. Am I still eating too much? Eating too much is when you get up from the table feeling 'as full as a tick'. Also remember to check your fat intake. Do not eat more than one type of fat per day if you are overweight. Remember, the more natural a fat the better it is for you – avocados and nuts are a better source of fat than butter, but butter is a better source of fat than margarine. Do not exclude natural fats from your diet altogether, as they contain the essential fatty acids that help your metabolic rate and hormonal system to function properly. Diets which prohibit fats are dangerous.

8. Can you see yourself slim? Lie in bed each night before going to sleep, and 'see' the new slim you. Visualise yourself with more energy and eating only healthful foods. It's vitally important for the successful attainment of your goal weight to be able to see yourself as 'you want to be'.

9. Don't ever compare yourself with other people. You are unique, one-of-a-kind. Your bone structure is unique, your metabolism is unique and so are your genes. Compete with yourself, not with the world.

Remember, if you have abused your body by going on and off various diets, it will take a while to rectify your metabolism. In the meantime, exercise regularly, start your day with some fruit, include raw vegetables with all meals other than fruit meals, combine your food correctly, and start to renew your mind by reading and learning more about your health. Banish all refined foods, additives, coffee, vinegar, onion and garlic from your diet. Keep yourself busy. But most importantly, remember that the Natural Way programme is not a diet or a religion, it is a life-style and it takes time to alter the habits of a lifetime.

If your problem is the opposite, that is if you are too thin and cannot gain weight, it is often a lot more difficult to correct. People with a slender build are usually genetically predisposed to thinness and are unlikely to become well-rounded.

But all is not lost, there are several steps you can take to pad yourself out a little, however, a few things need to be clarified first.

A change to the Natural Way programme usually results in weight loss, and this applies equally to those who are overweight at the outset and those who are underweight. This is the result of your body working through a catabolic phase, that is a breaking down of unhealthy tissue. This process could take anything from two weeks to a year before the metabolism stabilises and no further weight is lost. You may find this unwanted weight loss frustrating, particularly if you have increased your food intake in order to gain weight. But eating huge quantities at every meal during the catabolic phase could, ironically, cause further weight loss. The body is placed under unnecessary strain and cannot break the food down efficiently resulting in poor absorption of nutri-

108

ents. It would be better to eat smaller portions more frequently.

As always, listen to your body. Concentrate on increasing the proportion of high energy value food in your diet – avocados, dates (and all other dried fruits), bananas and natural unprocessed starches such as potatoes, brown rice and mealies (corn on the cob) are all suitable. By eating small portions of high energy food more often, you will find that you will experience a gradual weight gain. Also increase the quantity of fruit in your diet. Try eating less salad – salad is a negative energy food as it requires more energy from the body for digestion than it in fact gives to the body after digestion. By adding some cold-pressed oil to your salads you will increase their energy value significantly.

After the stabilisation phase which could last up to a year, your body will go through a rebuilding or anabolic phase. However, you will only experience this when your body is ready; it cannot be rushed along. Fasting under strict supervision is the only way to speed up the process of catabolism, stabilisation and anabolism.

Exercise such as weight training or resistance work done under the guidance of a qualified instructor can help to build your body in all the right places. However, you do need to be diligent about your training and keep it up until you see results.

If you still battle to gain weight after following these suggestions, console yourself with the fact that thinner people generally live a longer, healthier life and experience less strain on joints and organs.

Remember to focus on getting well and try not to be distracted by either weight gain or weight loss. In time your body will function at its optimum level, regardless of whether you have a sleek or a nicely rounded shape. Your ultimate reward will be glowing health, loads of energy and peace of mind.

CHAPTER FIFTEEN

Mainly for Men

BY MARK SHEARER

I have always loved food! As far back as I can remember, I have enjoyed eating, and for my sins, I ended up in the restaurant business as well. With this thought in mind, let me tell you why I am writing a chapter in Mary-Ann's book and how 'painless' the transition was for the husband of South Africa's Healthiest Woman (sic).

For us the change to the Natural Way life-style was significant. The key to understanding and accepting this sort of change is 'knowledge' (to use the title of a book by Len J Jones, *Ignorance is Not Bliss*), and if knowledge is the key, then desperation is the driving force.

Mary-Ann and I were desperate for some answers, answers backed by common sense and sound reasoning. Not the 'do as I say, because I'm a doctor' sort of answer. We needed to understand our bodies, especially as we knew that God in His wisdom did not make us with grommets in our ears and nor did He design us to rely on any of the thousands of superficial remedies available through medical science today.

On with my story. Mary-Ann and I married in the January of 1977. I was working for Kentucky Fried Chicken as an assistant manager then, and I have worked in hotels and restaurants ever since. I have always thought of myself as being healthy, but not-as-fit-as-I-could-be sort of thing, having played active sport all my school and army life. But two maladies bothered me from seventeen or eighteen years of age – severe indigestion and high blood pressure. These were explained as 'inherited' from my parents; my Dad suffered the indigestion continually, and my Mum had the blood pressure problem. It irritated the hell out of me that I was penalised for having 'high blood-pressure' by the insurance companies when I had hardly started shaving the teenage fuzz from my cheeks! Anyway, life goes on, and I had to live with the fact that every time I had my blood-pressure taken, it was 'elevated' for my age-group and weight, and that there was nothing I nor anyone else could do about it.

Well, if you too believe that there are no solutions to these problems, let me tell you that you are wrong. These conditions are very easily explained and equally easily rectified, and if you have the interest and resolve necessary to have gotten this far in this book, you're okay pal!

During 1984 to 1985, the desperate years for us and our daughters, I came across and bought the book, *Food Combining for Health*. We were at this time eating all the 'health' foods around; I was off coke and white bread, and into 'bran' in a Big way (I used to take tablespoons of the stuff and stir it into a glass of milk and force myself to drink this tasteless, coarse gunge), and despite all these radical precautions, we still managed to catch every flu, whether of the local or imported variety, and my youngest (now middle!) daughter had the proverbial 'glazed doughnut' face constantly. And Mary-Ann was destroying our sleep with her sneezing, rashes and her interminable post nasal drip.

The long and the short of it is that we put the principles of food combining into practice and things started to change. And how they changed! My indigestion disappeared! Never to return (except when I cheat) and Mary-Ann's many maladies cleared up within days. That was the beginning of

111

what I refer to as my first 'realization' that there is more to diet than just feeding our faces.

I'm not going to rewrite Mary-Ann's book, as all is basically said and done, but let me add that as a man, and a husband and a father, you need your energy. Energy is the secret to success. Without it nothing gets done. No new ideas get implemented and no risks are taken. And without risk, no meaningful change or venture can be achieved, no goals can be reached, and, the bottom-line is, no 'real' orgasm can be had!

Jokes aside, sex is really important to most men, and the change to my diet resulted in improved performance and pleasure. But if the transition to this life-style has done anything for me, it has given me energy. It has also helped me to understand the body that I will have to live in for the rest of my life. It helped me to understand why I would on occasions get unexplainable anxiety attacks. When I had cleansed my system by eating correctly, I was able to isolate coffee as the culprit. I don't get these attacks any more, and believe me, I work in a stressful environment. Today, I can have a cup of coffee, I can have a beer, a glass of wine or even a whisky (ugh!) if I so choose, but I never have more than two, simply because I am not prepared to spend a week (and I'm not joking) recovering from the after effects.

As far as the ubiquitous business lunch is concerned, it is very easy to say 'I will stick to this or that' or 'no dressing for me'. These days colleagues are far less concerned when you have a 'light' lunch than they were some years ago. Restaurants too are far more accommodating about 'awkward' requests, so don't let that put you off. Most importantly, don't let your peers put you down! They won't ride the ambulance with you when you have your first heart attack.

How does the business man cope on the Natural Way programme? When I first switched over to this life-style, I would on occasion eat fish or chicken as part of my main meal. I have since lost the taste for animal flesh and now prefer to meet my protein requirements by starting the average day with ¼ to ½ cup of nuts eaten with acid fruit. I start with a glass of freshly-squeezed orange juice at about ten in the morning. (The type of juice varies according to the seasons; it may well be liquidized mango or pineapple at other times of the year.) About an hour later, I might have something more substantial like bananas and dates, or dates with apples (these are fresh dates, not the pressed, cooking dates) or even some cashews and oranges, or bananas and stewed prunes. This lasts me through until lunchtime or even dinnertime when I'll have a properly combined meal and plenty of it! If I know that I'm going to have to eat two cooked meals in a day, then I will not have anything other than the juice in the morning. For lunch (that is a working or business lunch) I'll have a salad (no dressing, no onion!) with a large baked potato with butter, and the vegetables of the day. (You may find it difficult at first to do without meat, in which case you could start with the salad and then go on to fish or steak of your choice – no chips or baked potato – and vegetables.) If I find that I have to attend a function where there will be a few drinks before a dinner, I decide beforehand whether I will be sticking to protein or carbohydrates, and that makes the choice through the evening a lot simpler. So if I decide to have carbohydrates, I could safely have beer or sweet wines. If I go the protein route, then the dry wines are the best bet. Fortunately, or perhaps unfortunately, I'm not sure which, spirits fit somewhere in the middle, so you whisky drinkers are pretty safe there. Remember that all of this rigmarole becomes second-nature once you understand the basics of food combination and have experienced the benefits of properly digested food.

Mary-Ann handles making the transition to the Natural Way life-style elsewhere in the book, but I feel that it is important to stress that the wake-up to lunch cycle should not be disturbed. I have found through bitter experience that a big breakfast or toast and coffee before noon will set me back for days. Business breakfasts are becoming increasingly popular these days. If you have to attend a working breakfast at any stage, start with fresh fruit first, then sit back and listen or talk for half an hour before you eat something else. Broaden that gap for better digestion where you can.

Look, there is going to have to be a certain amount of experimentation on your part, but the important thing is to grasp the principles fully. If you go off the rails once in a while, it is not a train smash; you just get back on track as soon as you can.

I find that exercising in the morning does wonders. Firstly, you don't particularly feel like eating much after a good workout so you can avoid the eating-too-much-too-early trap. Secondly, regular exercise is essential for vibrant health and tip-top energy levels. Today I walk between twenty and fifty kilometres a week and I try to spend time at the gym three to four nights a week (depending on my business schedule) and even if I miss a week or two due to injury or poor weather, I am able to resume my programme where I left off without any ill effects.

And remember guys, it is not just the length of our lives that is at stake here, it is the quality. Fewer ailments and aches and pains mean more productivity, and more productivity means more time for recreation and your family.

CHAPTER SIXTEEN

Making the Transition

By now you are probably in a tizz. 'Where do I start?' I can hear you say. The following chapter will, I'm sure, help you to make the transition as painlessly as possible. The key to changing your present, toxic dietary life-style to one that is conducive to energy and health is not to try changing overnight. It is a rare individual who can do away with life-long eating habits overnight and never look back. These few are to be commended. For the rest of us, a slow, gradual change is the answer.

Those of you who can make a total change immediately, might find that for the first week or two you feel very tired. You may also find that your stomach is either upset or constipated, or that you have headaches. In fact, you may even develop strong flu-like symptoms. It is best not to take any medication for these symptoms, however, but rather to rest and get to bed as early as possible. These unpleasant reactions are merely due to your having cut stimulants like tea or coffee out of the diet or any other non-food toxic substance and it is the body's way of purging itself of residual toxins. In my experience, very few people have any of these symptoms for longer than seven days, although most only suffer for a day or two. This is one of the reasons so few people jump in with both feet and prefer rather to make gradual changes. If you do get any of these symptoms you are not dying, only detoxifying! Take it slowly until you feel better.

Here follow some hints for making the change without experiencing too much stress.

THIS IS NOT A DIET, IT IS A LIFE-STYLE

Do not think of this way of eating as a diet. A 'diet' is something you start and then stop a while later. This is a new lifestyle that you are moving into. One cannot change a life-style overnight.

KNOW THAT A LIFELONG LIFE-STYLE CANNOT BE CHANGED OVERNIGHT

'Old habits die hard' is a most appropriate cliché at this point. The worst thing that you can do is to feel guilty about not being able to change your whole way of life overnight. Determine from the beginning that it is going to take some time, at least six months and maybe even a couple of years before you feel totally comfortable with your new way of life and altered eating patterns. But take heart, you will start feeling the benefits immediately, or at least after two weeks. Some people only start responding positively to a change in diet after a two-week period of cleansing and detoxification. Do not get despondent if you suffer from the unpleasant symptoms of detoxification. This is the last time you'll ever feel like this again!

WITH EACH MONTH THAT PASSES, STRIVE TO IMPROVE YOUR OVERALL DIET

Make up your mind that with each month that passes, your diet will be a little better than it was the previous month. Even if that only means that instead of eating pizza every other night, you now eat it every third night. Small improvements lead to more complete health. You are the better for it, no matter how gradual the change.

116

THIS IS NOT A 'GIVE-UP' DIET IT IS AN 'ADD-TO' DIET

Do not think in terms of sacrificing – 'I have to give up this and that – all the things I enjoy so much. I would rather eat the way I want to and die sick, but happy'. The emphasis should be on adding to the diet – adding more raw fruits and vegetables, rather than giving up the acid-forming 'good' foods you presently enjoy. As the body chemistry changes, your desires and cravings for foods will also change. Smokers often respond to this change by no longer feeling like a cigarette – to their amazement.

KNOW THAT WRONG CRAVINGS WILL EVENTUALLY BE FEWER AND FARTHER APART

As you gradually, but steadily, improve your diet, the body chemistry will begin to improve. The result will be that your desire for stimulation (toxic foods) will decrease just as gradually. Instead of craving pizzas three times a week, it will be just twice a week. Once you have been adding more fruits and vegetables to your diet for some time, your cravings for other foods will be less frequent.

CRAVINGS FOR GOOD FOODS WILL INCREASE WITH TIME

No matter how boring the very thought of a predominantly raw fruit and vegetable diet may seem, know that as the body chemistry changes towards a more alkaline, healthy chemistry, your desires and cravings for fresh and raw food will continually increase. These foods will become more palatable and you will wonder how you ever managed without them.

EAT AS WELL AS YOU CAN, FOR AS LONG AS YOU CAN

You may get really motivated to follow the diet. You get started, you do well for three days, and then an overwhelming craving for a pizza hits you. If you can resist, great! If you can't, eat the pizza, and the next day get back on the diet for as many days as you can until a craving takes over again. I find that the three-day-craving rule is a great help. Try putting off what you are craving for three days – if you still feel like it on the third day, you deserve it! Take care that you do not over-indulge. It is not worth it.

DO NOT FEEL GUILTY FOR NOT STICKING TO THE LIFE-STYLE 100%

The worst thing you can do, literally worse than not eating the right foods, is to feel guilty when you break the life-style because of an old craving. Keep in mind that you cannot change a life-style, you cannot change a body chemistry, overnight. Apply this rule to exercise as well. If you don't make it today, don't feel guilty – go for a walk with your dog or do some sit-ups, and get out and work at it the following day. I find that having a rebounder is a great help. After a couple of minutes of good bouncing, I feel that I have at least done some worthwhile exercise in the day.

A REWARD SYSTEM IS OFTEN BENEFICIAL

Some people have found that they can stick to the diet more diligently by making deals with themselves – 'once a week (month), I will have a splurge, I will eat anything I want, but for the rest of the time, I will follow the diet exactly'. Taking the family to a restaurant once a month and giving them the run of the menu, so to speak, is very effective. Over the years I have watched my family make healthier and healthier choices without any pressure on them to do so. This works particularly well if you are changing the eating patterns of the whole family. But don't overdo it. Just remember that the healthier you become, the less you will need these splurges, and the worse you will feel afterwards. Every indulgence will have its price.

DON'T BE TOO STUPID TO GET WELL

If you feel terrible after a splurge, or if you wake up with a 'hangover' the next morning, know that your body is now too healthy to tolerate certain foods. Continuing to splurge and getting sick afterwards is an act of total stupidity, and good health will be slow in following. Listen to your body and make the changes it needs.

LOOK BACK CONTINUALLY

What we tend to do when changing our eating patterns is to look forward to how far we still have to go. This can be most discouraging. Rather, take time, once a month, to look back at how far you have come. Take stock of how much your over-all diet has improved since you first began eating more healthily. This is most encouraging and motivating and it will help you to stay on track.

DO NOT STOCK THE FRIDGE AND PANTRY WITH NO-NO's

If toxic foods are not readily available, they are not so easily eaten. If you have to make a special effort to run down to the grocery store in the middle of the night to get ice-cream or chocolates, you may be deterred. This is a helpful suggestion for households that are attempting to change the children's diet; if the junk isn't in the house, they can't eat it. If they want it, they must provide their own transportation and money to get it. This is so important as they learn that they can take responsibility for what they eat.

DO NOT BECOME A MARTYR OR A FANATIC

Nothing is more off-putting than a fanatic – one who says, 'Look at me, I'm different and what's more, I'm better than you'. Neither do people care for a martyr whose message is,

'Poor me, I'm making the supreme sacrifice of diet to improve my health. Don't you feel sorry for me?' Both of these approaches reflect an attitude of pride and are counter-productive as people will be irritated both by you and your diet. In turn, this sort of negative feedback will discourage you and you may be tempted to give up the whole thing. Rather, don't be afraid to socialise and to eat a wrong thing or two now and then. Know instead that as time goes on and as this diet becomes more a part of you, your different life-style will not be offensive to others. It may become a point of interest and curiosity rather than one of irritation. Never give advice if you are not asked for it – ask me, I know!

HOW TO CONVERT AN UNWILLING FAMILY TO HEALTHFUL EATING

In the case of the mother (or cook) wanting to make the change of life-style, the best approach is not to warn the family that they are about to find strange, new meals on their plates. (The exception of course is if the family already has an excellent, above-average level of communication and if the children are very responsive to authority.) A subtle approach works far better. Without comment, over a period of months, ensure that the meals gradually become more nutritious. In addition to the regular meat serving, introduce lightly steamed vegetables and tossed green salad. Ensure that fewer dairy products, fried foods, red meats, pre-prepared foods and canned foods appear on the table. The most important step is to start by cutting out all brands of foods containing preservatives and other additives. This is essential.

The next step is to serve a meal without meat or dairy products once or twice a week. Make no comment about the omission, just sit down and carry on as usual. If you do comment, you could find strong resistance. Just take it slowly. You will find that this gradual approach will ensure that even the most reluctant family members will become accustomed to the new, healthier habits in time.

In the case where Mom and Dad agree on the diet change, the transition is much smoother. Still, the less fanfare the better. Just introduce more nutritious menus slowly, and set a good example by eating and enjoying without negative comment. Rather make positive comments about how good the vegetables taste as they are being eaten, and how good they are for the body. If questions are raised as to why the menus are different, be honest and direct, 'We've been reading (or the doctor told us, or John and Mary have been telling us) that junk foods makes our bodies sick'. I have found that by apologising to the children for having fed them junk, actually earned more respect. Follow with statements on how much better you have been feeling since eating properly, and comment on any change noticed in the children's health or behaviour with the improved diet. Don't neglect an opportunity to point out to the children when a slip away from healthful eating results in direct negative physical discomfort, both in you – 'Boy, that ice-cream sure gave me a headache', and in them – 'Johnny, see how you are acting since you've eaten that cake'. Remember to remove all artificially preserved and coloured foods, then introduce a bit of raw food at each meal. At breakfast start with a small fruit salad followed by their 'normal' breakfast. Eventually they will say that they are full from the fruit and will give the cereal or eggs a miss. Cut a few slices of tomato or avocado or carrot sticks and serve this with each meal as a slow introduction to raw food. I find that strips of raw vegetables (carrots, celery, cucumber and baby marrows) served with mashed avocado before a meal, are enjoyed by the whole family, and in particular by the children.

HINTS ON SOCIALISING WITHOUT OFFENDING YOUR HEALTH OR YOUR FRIENDS

You may find that once you and your family have made the

adjustment to the Natural Way life-style, you all cope very well in the home. But what happens when a social situation arises?

How to eat at a restaurant

Restaurants can be a veritable minefield of potential problems, but there is no need to sabotage your health or to spoil your fun. Always start with a fresh salad, and ask the waiter to leave the dressing off as it is extremely acidic. If you like a tang to your salad, ask for plain oil and a fresh lemon and use this instead of the usual dressing. Try to order foods that are the least acidic and try to eat meals in good combination. Order salad and baked potato, or salad and fish, or even just salad. Go for the neutral veggies or choose a pasta dish. If comments are made, say, 'I'm just not that hungry, thank you'. Don't be afraid to say, 'It looks good, but I'm trying to change my life-style and it is making me feel so much better'.

How to be a good guest

Sharing a meal with friends need not be a source of panic. At potluck dinners, go for the salads and vegetables. Who's going to notice? When sitting around a table, take the smallest portions and try to combine correctly. If you are planning to have the dessert, stick to carbohydrates during the main course – your stomach can handle this combination better than that of a protein followed by dessert. The most important rule to remember in a social setting is that quantity always outweights quality. If you are in a position where you cannot avoid eating toxic foods or poor combinations, one helping will do. The body can, without too much cost, handle the occasional binge if the digestive system is not overloaded. However, what we tend to do when the opportunity arises, is to eat far too much. It is actually harder on the body to overload in this manner than to eat incorrectly but moderately every day.

How to entertain healthily

When inviting others to your home, keep it simple. Fortunately there is a strong move away from rich complicated catering, not only at home but also in restaurants. It has in fact become quite fashionable to be health-conscious.

When planning your menu, it is best to cater for yourself first and then for your guests. In other words, let the focus of the meal be on alkaline-forming dishes such as salads and vegetables rather than having the table groaning with meat dishes. (Even the World Health Organisation says that animal products should be regarded as the condiments to a meal.) If you must have a barbecue, go to town on the salads and try to serve only one kind of meat. A Mongolian barbecue is the ideal compromise. Prepare mounds of vegetables of your choice, including mushrooms, red peppers, bean sprouts, carrots and celery by cutting them into thin strips suitable for stir-frying. In addition, you could also prepare the meat or chicken beforehand by slicing it into thin strips as well. Then all you need for a successful barbecue is a large flat cooking surface, heated from below. A 'skottelbraai' or wok-shaped barbecue dish is ideal. Guests then proceed to 'cook' their own meals by stir-frying whatever combination they like. This is a very sociable form of entertaining and it is a very easy way to stick to good combinations. Vegetables done on or in the fire are delicious as well. Our favourite is potato done in foil. I wrap the potatoes in wax-wrap first (this prevents contamination of the food by aluminium) then in foil. Other vegetables we enjoy prepared in this way are mealies, broccoli, fresh asparagus, butternut and mushrooms. Add a bit of butter or cold pressed olive oil and some seasoning of your choice, and it's quite delicious. In fact you don't even need meat at a barbecue to enjoy the occasion.

123

Our favourite evenings are spent with friends around the table enjoying a properly combined meal. To give you some idea of how to go about this, here is a brief description of what I might serve for a casual supper.

When serving snacks or a starter, I go for crudités (fresh vegetables such as carrots and cucumber cut into strips) served with a dip. We prefer avocado dips although a ricotta cheese based dip is also quite nice and a brinjal or mushroom pâté is even nicer. We might also serve some plain salted crisps with the dips. (Crisps are deep fried and therefore not ideal, but as a cheat for special occasions they pass.)

Our main course is more often than not a pasta and vegetable dish (a better combination than pasta and meat), always accompanied by a large fresh salad. I might serve a loaf of freshly-baked bread with this, together with butter cut into cubes (the girls love doing this for me). In fact we try to include our children in the preparation of all our meals, with Mark making the salad, the girls setting the table, cutting the butter, slicing the crudités and making the dip, and with me as the director and maker of the main course. This way I know that they will grow up knowing how to entertain and how to prepare food properly. If you have sons, involve them in the kitchen. You will be surprised at how they love it. With the pasta dish I sometimes serve a bowl of grated Parmesan or Pecorino cheese for sprinkling, restaurant-style, on top. Although this is not ideal from a food combining point of view, it does add that little bit extra to the meal and it won't cause too much harm. Those who are dairy intolerant, should skip the cheese.

Dessert after any meal is not ideal as it usually has a high sugar content which, on top of the rest of your meal, will ferment in your stomach. If you serve dessert, a simple one free of preservatives and colourants is best. Dessert tends to ferment less when eaten after a starch, as opposed to a protein, meal. Serving dessert is not obligatory these days, but if you feel that you must, remember that the simpler the dessert, the better. I often place a bowl of fresh dates on the table instead of after dinner mints.

For a casual lunch we serve various breads with rye or wholewheat crackers and dips, and of course plenty of salads. Wholewheat pita bread stuffed with salad is a firm favourite.

A more formal dinner could consist of a vegetable starter such as steamed asparagus and hollandaise sauce or lemon butter, or grilled black mushrooms, plain or stuffed with any mixture of vegetables. Avocado is a winner. Half an avocado scooped out and mashed or cubed with tomato, olives, celery and feta cheese also goes down well. Alternatively, stuffed fresh tomatoes are a light, tasty starter. Just scoop out the flesh, dice it and mix with fresh chopped basil, salt and pepper, feta cheese and olives, and return the mixture to the shell.

The main course would always have a fresh, crisp salad including any and every vegetable you like. Lightly steamed vegetables such as broccoli, cauliflower and mushrooms are always interesting and tasty. Serve these with grilled sole or kingklip. Grill the fish on a bakingsheet. Dot with butter, drizzle with freshly-squeezed lemon or lime juice, and sprinkle with salt and pepper. Grill for approximately 15 minutes. Or you could serve spinach and mushroom stuffed buckwheat pancakes instead of the fish (see *The Natural Way Recipe Book II*).

So you see, entertaining at home the Natural Way is easy. Remember to keep it simple, spend time making the table attractive and present the food with love and care. Little sprigs of parsley or fresh herbs, or twists of lemon or cucumber always show that you care just that little bit more.

How to cater for a children's party

I find that many mothers battle with children's parties, but

125

with a little lateral thinking, you will find that an ice-cream cake, fizzy cooldrinks and brightly coloured sweets and biscuits need not be the only option.

Popcorn is popular with any age group. Using a dry popper is best, but cold-pressed sunflower oil is fine provided you resort to this method of preparation only on the odd occasion. (Remember that heated fats are not all that good for the body.) A light sprinkling of herbal salt and you're away! Plain salted crisps, although not ideal, can also be served. Go for the unflavoured crisps as one never knows exactly what is used in the 'flavouring'. Unsalted, unroasted nuts are a good savoury alternative, and bowls of cashews, almonds, pecans or macadamias are a great treat for any child.

On the sweet side, a good carrot cake is a winner, and for birthday parties it can be cut into any number of shapes and iced. (See recipe in the next chapter.) Carob cake is a good alternative to the usual chocolate cake and is of course, much healthier. (See recipe for Pet's Devil Food cake.) Dates, raisins and unbleached sultanas are also popular. Of course, oat crunchies always go down well. I have included a gluten free recipe in the next chapter as well as one containing wheat flour. They are both delicious. Date and coconut balls are a lot of fun and tasty too. (See recipe.) You can indulge occasionally and have 'real sweets', but go for those containing no preservatives or artificial colouring.

A great way to start the party is to set out bowls of fruit salad or trays arranged with a variety of colourful fruits cut into squares. Include some toothpicks for the fun of it.

Have the trays ready as the children arrive, and once they have eaten the fruit, let them play for a while before you bring out the other goodies. (This will allow the fruit to digest before they tuck into the rest of the food.)

Whole rye or wholewheat breads and biscuits as well as pita bread are more substantial snacks. They are also suitable for theme parties with a Western, or American flavour.

Although hotdogs are out, home-made pizzas with or without cheese (see recipes), corn on the cob and tacos (preservative and additive free) filled with a salad, are filling and nourishing. Set out some wholewheat rolls with cubed butter, grated uncoloured cheese, large grilled black mushrooms, mashed avocados, tomato slices and lettuce, and let them make their own 'properly combined' hamburgers using the mushroom as the 'patty'. (Include the cheese for those who don't eat mushrooms).

Instead of the usual fizzy cooldrinks, serve juices that are free of preservatives or added sugar. Ice-cream can be served if you must, but look for a fairly 'pure' brand or make your own. Caramel ice-cream is easy to make and is always popular. Take a large tin of caramel and 500 ml cream (or 250 ml cream and 250 ml milk), and blend together in your food processor. Freeze the mixture for a couple of hours until set, remove and blend again. Refreeze and remove and blend once more. Freeze once again. Serve when frozen and you will agree, it is delicious! Although this is an additive-free treat, it is very high in animal fat and refined sugar, neither of which is particularly good for the body.

Parties don't have to be complicated. I have often prepared far too many dishes, realising afterwards that a more simple approach would have been better. So often we don't want to deviate from the norm and end up serving the usual hotdogs, hamburgers and ice-cream. Be daring, be different, be first! I have yet to see children not enjoying a 'healthy' party. Keep thinking laterally and you'll come up with some great healthy ideas! (For more sugar-, wheat- and egg-free dishes see *The Natural Way Recipe Books I* and *II.*)

You will find it rather difficult to combine correctly at a children's party. Just do your best and get back on track the next day. So often we think that if we can't combine properly we might as well go the whole way and just serve total junk. Try to stick to the basic Natural Way principles, and you will find that there will be no unpleasant repercussions.

FOOD GRADING CRITERIA

I have found that being able to grade food is very helpful when trying to decide which sorts of foods are healthier than others. In other words, by using the food grading criteria, you will be able to see that a baked potato is far healthier than a roasted one and you will be able to make the best decisions for your health when faced with a choice. It is a simple and effective system which will be of great benefit to you when making the transition to the Natural Way programme.

Food grading – the ABC of foods

All foods can be graded into four simple categories.

A foods – these are fresh, raw and whole (whole foods are those in their natural state). Seventy-five per cent of the diet should be made up of these foods which include all fresh fruit and vegetables. In other words, seventy-five per cent of your food budget should be spent at the greengrocer.

B Foods – these have only two criteria. For example, baked potato is fresh and whole, but not raw.

C Foods – these are only fresh, only raw or only whole. In other words, they have one criterion only. For example, unpolished rice is whole, but not fresh or raw.

D Foods – these have none of the above criteria. For example, crisps are neither whole, nor raw nor fresh. Even within the D foods group there are healthier choices whole-wheat bread is better than white bread, and oat and coconut biscuits are better than shop-bought centre-filled biscuits.

BUYING, STORING AND PREPARATION OF REAL FOOD

Once food grading has become second-nature to you, and once you have made the best choices for your health, you must ensure that you do not destroy valuable nutrients inadvertently by the incorrect storage and preparation of your food. Here are some helpful tips to ensure that you derive the most benefit from your diet.

1 Buy produce as close to ripe as possible. It is cheaper and you know that it will ripen properly.

2 Do not buy foods that will not rot as these contain a preservative of some kind. Long shelf-life foods should also be avoided for the same reason.

3 Do not buy foods that have been irradiated. Irradiation has been shown to cause carcinogenic and mutagenic changes in foodstuffs, as well as to destroy vital nutrients – avoid them.

4 Do not buy foods that contain any additives, including colourants and artificial flavourants.

5 Buy foods as close to their natural state as possible, for example don't buy any ready-peeled vegetables or pre-prepared salads.

6 Wash or scrub your fruits and vegetables carefully to remove any residual fertilizers or insecticides.

7 Store vegetables that don't have skins (such as lettuce and cabbage) in air-tight containers or plastic bags.

8 Steaming is the best way to cook – this method destroys the least nutrients.

9 Waterless cooking is second-best.

10 Stir-frying is a good method if water instead of oil is used. This is done very easily and effectively.

11 Roasting and baking are also good methods of preparation as there is no water involved to carry away nutrients. Bear in mind though that extreme temperatures can destroy some nutrients.

12 Avoid boiling as it robs food of nutrients.

13 Avoid aluminium foil and pots, and Teflon-coated cookware. These substances oxidise easily, contaminating the food during the cooking process and can get into the bloodstream.

14 Avoid all fried foods. The body cannot cope with heated fats.
15 Try not to use a microwave oven – this method of cooking destroys as many nutrients as pressure cooking or vigorous boiling. Then there is always the danger of leakage.
16 Use as few condiments as possible.

Making the transition from your old habits to the Natural Way life-style is not as difficult or as complicated as you may have feared. Take things slowly and don't become discouraged if you are not able to progress as quickly as you would like. Try to stick to the Natural Way principles whenever you can – turning to the hints and suggestions outlined in this chapter will be of encouragement and will help you to stay on track. As far as your new eating patterns are concerned – keep it simple, keep it healthy and *bon appétit!*

CHAPTER SEVENTEEN

Cooking up a Storm: The Natural Way

...r are suitable for a family of five ...joy our food and are particular-...h Mark hankering after his Dur-...ain. These meals are intended to ...as tasty and healthy. Any of the ...or increased or decreased – just ...nily's taste, life-style and pock-...at these are by no stretch of the ...s. The idea behind them is to ...ing healthy food. Anyone in the ...pare these dishes. Mark and the ...ake any of these meals, and they

...s into neutral, starch and protein ...a properly combined meal easy. ...either with starch or protein, or ...ir own. Starch dishes should be ...bine well with any neutral veg-...ine well with salads and neutral ...rches.

...ction small deliberately as any ...cooked as simply as possible, ...d preferably without added fat.

131

Thin slivers of fish, chicken or meat can be added to any neutral dish, including the salads, to make a protein meal.

When cooking Natural Way meals, you will find that you spend far less time in the kitchen, and that you enjoy your time there far more. Enjoy the foods God created by doing as little to them as possible. Remember to keep the dishes simple and to start each cooked, non-fruit meal with something raw. (For more recipes see *The Natural Way Recipe Books I* and *II*.) You will find that you will be spending more time at the greengrocer, and for this reason, it is important to find a good one who is willing to accommodate your needs and wishes.

If you have any difficulty in finding any of the ingredients or utensils mentioned in the book, please feel free to contact me (my address appears at the back of the book).

Good luck and enjoy yourself!

FRUITS

The best way to eat any fruit is in its whole state, but to make your breakfast a bit more interesting you might like to try some of these suggestions. Remember to buy fruit in season. Not only is it cheaper, but it tastes far nicer too. Summer fruits include mangoes, litchis, grapes, watermelons, peaches, nectarines, apricots, cherries, strawberries and plums, while the winter fruits are oranges, naartjies, pawpaws, kiwi fruit, guavas, apples and pears. Although many of these fruits are available all year round, they are often kept in cold storage for up to nine months. Oranges and apples in particular are stored in this way. Flavour is lost during storage and the cores are often bad. Bananas are available all year round.

Ideas for blended fruit shakes

Blended shakes are a delicious and easy way to get reluctant fruit-eaters to turn to fruit with relish. Remember that although the fruits are blended and served in a glass, these

shakes are a food and should be sipped slowly.
- *Mango and pineapple (add a couple of granadillas if you wish)*
- *Mango and nectarine*
- *Mango and peach*
- *Pawpaw, banana and dates*
- *Mango and banana*

In fact, if you blend any of the sub-acid fruits with acid fruits, or any sub-acid fruits with sweet fruits, you are sure to have a delicious Fruit Shake. The same principle applies to fruit salad combinations. Here you could add some dates, raisins or sultanas to any sweet fruit combination.

NEUTRAL DISHES

These dishes should be served either with a protein or a starch, or they can be enjoyed on their own.

Salads

Salads always form the most important part of the meal. They should be fun, tasty and should appear on the table every day. Even at a restaurant, salad should still form part of the meal. Here I refer specifically to fresh salad, not to cooked salads. If there are cooked ingredients in a salad, try to add as many other raw ingredients as possible. Remember that there is far more goodness in raw ingredients than in cooked.

In our family, avocados are a staple salad ingredient. But avocado pears are a much maligned fruit. Mention that you eat avocados and people throw up their hands in horror with shrieks of 'fattening' and 'cholesterol'. Let's get one thing straight, there is not a single fruit or vegetable which is able to manufacture cholesterol – this process is confined to the animal kingdom (see chapter on fats). Although avocados do contain fats, they are unsaturated fats which are easy to digest and which contain essential fatty acids which help the hormonal system to function properly.

Avocados are also extremely nutritious, containing 14 minerals, 11 vitamins and a high percentage of protein for a fruit. (Yes, avocado is a fruit although we do tend to eat it as a vegetable.)

Avocados are in season from late summer to the following mid-summer, which means that they are unobtainable for two months of the year only. I might add that this short period of deprivation makes Mark's life a misery. He can't bear salad without avocado and insists on adding olives to make it more interesting. Mark's favourite way of eating avocados is to have them mashed on hot, buttered toast. I like to use avocados as a skin treatment – I use the inside of the skin to rub on any dry patches. It is the most wonderful skin cream and has the added benefit of being completely natural.

A word of caution – if you are wanting to lose weight, don't eat more than one avocado per day. If on the other hand you are trying to gain some weight, try to eat at least three avocados every day.

Here is a recipe for our favourite salad (which contains avocado, of course). We adapt it in a number of ways and I have included the variations below.

Basic Avocado Salad

1 medium lettuce, broken into bite-size pieces
4 medium tomatoes, sliced or diced
4 medium avocados, diced
1 red pepper, sliced or chopped
2 sticks celery, chopped
1 tablespoon chopped parsley (optional)
2 carrots, cut into small strips

Toss all the ingredients together in a large salad bowl, and serve. The avocado makes this salad deliciously creamy. Add a bit of herbal salt and pepper to taste if you like. This salad can be served with either a protein or a starch meal, or inside wholewheat pita bread.

Variations on a theme

Any of the following ingredients can be added to the Basic Avocado Salad to ring the changes:

- *Olives in brine (not vinegar)*
- *Fresh, or tinned, asparagus tips*
- *Thin slices of chicken or meat*
- *Flaked tuna*
- *Feta cheese*
- *Cubed uncoloured cheese*
- *Chopped red cabbage*

Special note: If you add cheese, chicken, fish or meat to the salad, it is no longer a neutral dish but becomes a protein meal.

Avocado Starters

For a delicious and healthy start to any meal, serve avocado in the shell. Allow half an avocado per person, remove the pip and rub the flesh with lemon juice to prevent discoloration. Fill with any of the following mixtures:

Add home-made mayonnaise to:
- *Chopped chicken, chopped spring onion, sliced mushrooms, herbal salt, pepper and lemon juice (Protein meal)*
- *Asparagus pieces with chopped olives (Neutral meal)*
- *Grated uncoloured cheese and chopped spring onion (Protein meal)*

Add ricotta cheese to:
- *Chopped red pepper and olives (Protein or borderline neutral)*

– Chopped cucumber and celery seasoned with herbal salt
  and pepper (Protein or borderline neutral)

Add sour cream to:
– Slivers of smoked salmon and lemon juice (Protein meal)
– Flaked tuna, chopped chives and lemon juice (Protein
  meal)
– Chopped tomato, fresh basil and spring onion (Neutral
  meal)

Another way to serve the avocado would be to mash the flesh with any of the above fillings and to return the mixture to the shell, or to spoon it onto a lettuce leaf.

Special note: Try to eat only those vegetables which are in season. They are cheaper and tastier. Any good greengrocer will be able to tell you which vegetables are in season.

Avocado Sauces, Dressings and Dips

Avocado dips are a particularly good way of getting children to eat salad as they are often not all that fond of raw vegetables. Make up a platter of sliced raw vegetables – such as celery, baby marrow, steamed asparagus, carrots, tomatoes, red pepper or broccoli and cauliflower (either raw or lightly steamed) – and serve with one of the following dips:

– Avocado, tomato and fresh basil
– Avocado, tomato, red pepper and celery
– Avocado, sour cream, fresh lemon juice, herbal salt,
  black pepper and chopped chives
– Avocado, lemon juice, herbal salt and pepper

Blend the ingredients in a food processor and add a little filtered water if a more fluid salad dressing is required. The quantities and proportions of ingredients depends on your personal preferences. The blended dips (without additional water) are also suitable as sauces for dressing steamed vegetables, chicken or fish.

Coleslaw

½ white cabbage, shredded finely
1 small red cabbage, shredded finely
1 bunch spring onions, chopped
4 carrots, grated

Mix all ingredients together and add home-made mayonnaise or sour cream and seasoning to taste. (Shredding the ingredients with a food processor makes life a lot easier.)

Bean Sprout Salad

Variety of bean sprouts
Sliced mushrooms
Firm tomato wedges
Chopped celery

Mix ingredients thoroughly and toss in lemon juice.

Liz's Salad

Shredded cabbage
Bean sprouts or bamboo shoots
Chopped celery
Diced avocado

Combine almost equal quantities of the above ingredients and season, if you wish, with herbal salt and black pepper.

Sandy's Cauliflower Salad

2 small cauliflowers
1 large broccoli
2 punnets green beans

Stuffed green olives
Celery, sliced or chopped

Dressing:
Juice of 2 – 3 lemons
Herbal salt
1 – 2 tablespoons cold-pressed oil

Break the cauliflower and broccoli into small florets and steam, together with the green beans, for about 5 minutes. When cool, toss with remaining ingredients. Mix the dressing ingredients and pour over the salad.

Beetroot and Parsley Salad

500 g cooked beetroot
2 tablespoons chopped parsley
2 teaspoons grated orange rind

Dressing:
½ cup cold-pressed olive or sunflower seed oil
2 tablespoons lemon juice
1 teaspoon honey
Herbal salt and freshly ground black pepper to taste

Peel and dice the cooked beetroot. Combine the parsley and orange rind and mix with the beetroot. Combine all the dressing ingredients and toss through the salad. Reserve a little parsley and orange rind for decoration.

Special note: Lemon juice can destroy the starch digesting enzyme, ptyalin. Some people may find that their digestion is disturbed because of this. If you do have a problem, use lemon dressings on salad only when you are eating a protein meal.

Vegetables

Vegetables are generally at their nicest in winter, especially potatoes, butternut, broccoli, cauliflower and Brussels sprouts. Avocados are abundant in the winter and are very reasonably priced at this time of year. Vegetables are best eaten raw or lightly steamed. A stainless steel retractable steamer or a bamboo steamer are particularly efficient. The next best are frozen vegetables, followed by additive-free tinned varieties. As dried vegetables are usually treated with sulphur dioxide, it is best to avoid them.

Some Quick Ideas

– Take a punnet of broccoli and 1 small cauliflower, cut into small sprigs and steam for 5 – 10 minutes. Arrange in a dish in rings of contrasting colours. Dot with butter and squeeze some fresh lemon juice over the florets. Steamed button mushrooms added to this are also very tasty, and an avocado dip makes the dish something special.

– Steamed asparagus rolled in butter and drizzled with lemon juice is delicious, or serve with home-made mayonnaise to ring the changes.

– Brussels sprouts or fresh broccoli, steamed and served with butter and chopped mint or flaked almonds are a treat.

– Fresh garden peas, steamed and dotted with butter are good with chopped mint.

– Baby carrots (or julienne slices) steamed and tossed with chopped parsley and butter are very tasty.

– Thinly-sliced baby marrow steamed with button mushrooms and tossed in butter are always popular.

– Steamed broccoli tossed together with button mushrooms, diced avocado and sliced rings of red pepper is an unusual and delicious dish.

– Steamed spinach blended in a food processor with fresh cream, herbal salt and black pepper is excellent – Feta cheese can be used instead of the cream.

139

- Steamed button mushrooms and baby mealies are another favourite.
- Make a quick and delicious casserole by cutting a wide variety of seasonal vegetables into bite-size pieces and placing them in an oven-proof dish with 2 – 3 teaspoons of yeast extract and a little filtered water. Cover the dish and bake at 180°C for 50 minutes.
- Bake whole butternut at 160° C – 180° C for an hour. When done, cut the butternut in half lengthways and scoop out the pips. Serve with knobs of butter or stuff with brown rice or a vegetable mixture.

Vegetable Soup

Place any and as many different sorts of vegetables in a large pot and cover with 1 – 2 litres of water. Add 1 – 2 teaspoons of yeast extract or 1 MSG-free vegetable stock cube for flavour. Season with herbal salt and herbs of your choice. Potatoes or barley can be added, but bear in mind that the soup then becomes a starch meal.

Special note: When serving soup, do not forget to start with something raw. Remember that soup is a food and that it should be chewed or swirled in the mouth, and not just gulped down.

Mushroom Soup

2 tablespoons butter
1 small bunch spring onions, chopped finely
1 medium carrot, sliced
1 celery stalk, sliced
250 g mushrooms, sliced
1 heaped teaspoon yeast extract
2 – 3 cups filtered water
Nutmeg
Herbal salt
4 tablespoons thick cream

1 tablespoon dry sherry (optional)

Cook the chopped onion gently in butter over a low heat. Add the carrot, celery and mushrooms and toss in the butter. Add the yeast extract and water and simmer gently for about 15 minutes. Add seasoning and serve. Alternatively blend in a food processor, reheat and add the sherry, cream and a dash of nutmeg. This soup can be served with a salad and whole-wheat bread as a starch meal, or with salad and a protein.

Special note: Marmite can be used in cooking as it is a yeast extract free of artificial additives.

Aubergine Pâté

2 large aubergines (brinjals)
Juice of 1 lemon
40 ml cold-pressed sunflower seed oil
Herbal salt
2 tablespoons chopped parsley
1 bunch spring onions (optional)

Bake the aubergines at 160°C for 45 minutes. Peel off the skin and squeeze off any excess juice. Place in a food processor and blend with half the lemon juice and the onions. Add one tablespoon of oil. With the blender running, add the rest of the oil, the salt and the remaining lemon juice. Stir in the parsley, turn into a bowl and chill. Serve with crudités or wholewheat and rye crackers.

Creamed Spinach

1- 2 bunches fresh spinach
1 carton double cream
Herbal salt
Freshly ground black pepper
Dash of nutmeg

Blend steamed spinach in a food processor, fold in the rest of the ingredients and heat before serving.

Special note: If you want to turn this into a protein dish, add 100 g – 200 g of Feta cheese.

Quick and Simple Ratatouille

1 onion, chopped (optional – I prefer celery)
3 brinjals, sliced
1 punnet baby marrows, sliced
2 red peppers, sliced
1 punnet mushrooms, sliced (optional)
4 – 5 large tomatoes, peeled and chopped
Fresh origanum, chopped
Herbal salt to taste

Layer the ingredients in a casserole dish or saucepan, and either bake at 200°C for 30 minutes to an hour, or simmer gently on the stove.

Special note: As a variation, add a layer of sliced potato and make a starch meal of this dish.

Asparagus with à la King Sauce

2 punnets button mushrooms, sliced
½ bottle olives in brine, destoned and sliced
2 cans asparagus chunks
1 tablespoon butter
1 heaped tablespoon wholewheat or pea flour
250 ml cream or soya milk
500 g peas

Stir-fry mushrooms over medium heat without water or oil. Add the olives, asparagus chunks (reserve juice), peas, butter and enough flour to absorb the moisture. Add the asparagus juice, stirring all the time. Add cream and heat through.

Serve on its own with a fresh salad, or spoon over a bed of brown rice or eggless noodles for a starch meal. This dish is a good substitute for those who miss the 'bad' combination of Chicken à la King.

Savoury Mushrooms

2 – 3 punnets mushrooms (about 500 g)
Butter
Herbal salt
Nutmeg
Freshly ground pepper

Wash mushrooms carefully and place them whole in an oven-proof dish. Dot with butter, sprinkle with herbal salt, pepper and a dash of nutmeg, and bake for 15 – 20 minutes at 180° C. Serve as a main or side dish with a starch or other vegetables. Don't forget the salad.

Mushrooms Florentine

1 large black mushroom per person (starter)
or
2 – 3 large black mushrooms per person (main course)
Creamed spinach (see earlier recipe)

Steam or grill the mushrooms lightly. Spoon creamed spinach on top of each mushroom and add a sprinkling of Parmesan or crumbled Feta cheese if you want a protein meal. Pop back under the grill and garnish with tomato slices.

This dish is a good starter with some raw salad, or a filling main course if served with a starch or protein.

Vegetarian Mushroom Stew

250 g mushrooms
2 tablespoons cold-pressed sunflower seed or olive oil
1 bunch spring onion, chopped

700 g ripe tomatoes, chopped
2 red peppers, chopped
2 – 3 punnets baby marrows, sliced
Herbal salt
Freshly ground black pepper

Slice all the vegetables and sauté in a large saucepan. Simmer gently for 10 minutes, season and serve. This stew is good as a topping for baked potato or brown rice, and is equally good with fish or chicken.

Vegetable Curry

1 litre filtered water
6 teaspoons mixed curry powders (I have 3 different types
  and use 2 teaspoons of each)
2 teaspoons ground cumin
1 teaspoon cinnamon
1 teaspoon tumeric
1 teaspoon ground ginger
1 teaspoon coarse salt
1 teaspoon ground coriander
½ cup fresh lemon juice (optional)
1 – 2 kg mixed vegetables

Place all the ingredients (except the vegetables) in a large pot and bring to the boil. Reduce heat and simmer for about 30 minutes. Add a combination of vegetables such as broccoli, green beans, carrots, cauliflower, and simmer for a further 30 minutes to 1 hour. If you want a butternut curry, use 3 large cubed butternuts instead of the mixed vegetables. Serve with brown rice.

Special note: This recipe is sufficient for 8 to 10 servings. It keeps well and is delicious if served at a later stage – the flavours seem to mature.

Cucumber Sambal

1 English cucumber
1 tablespoon chopped mint
1 red pepper, seeded and finely chopped
1 bunch spring onions, finely chopped
⅔ cup sour cream
½ teaspoon herbal salt
Pinch cayenne pepper

Grate the unpeeled cucumber and squeeze the excess water from the pulp in a sieve. Mix in the remaining ingredients, cover and chill until needed. Serve with a vegetable curry and rice.

Banana Sambal

4 ripe bananas
4 tablespoons sour cream
2 tablespoons honey

Mix the honey and sour cream well. When blended, pour over the bananas to coat. Serve immediately with vegetable curry and rice.

Special note: Although it is not ideal to eat fruit with other foods, bananas or other sweet fruits can often be tolerated by the stomach when eaten with a starch. Do not, however, make a habit of this combination.

Tomato and Onion Sambal

3 large ripe tomatoes, diced
3 bunches spring onions, chopped
15 ml fresh lemon juice
Pinch cayenne pepper
5 ml soy sauce (MSG-free)
½ teaspoon herbal salt

Mix all ingredients and chill until needed. Serve with a vegetable curry and brown rice.

Roti

1 cup white bread flour
1 cup brown bread flour
1 tablespoon cold-pressed oil
1 cup water
Pinch sea salt

Mix the flour with the oil and the salt in a food processor. Add the water slowly and mix to form a soft, pliable dough. Divide into 4 or 8 equal portions, depending on the size required. Roll out each ball until it is as thin as a pancake. Brush with a little oil and place on a hot griddle or in a large frying pan. Turn over several times until cooked. Serve with a vegetable curry.

Special note: Although roti is served with a neutral vegetable curry, it is a starch dish. It can be made in advance, wrapped in wax paper and steamed until warm when needed. If a craving for pancakes overtakes you, spread the roti with honey and whipped cream, roll up and enjoy your 'cheat'.

Wheatgerm Stuffing

4 heaped teaspoons wheatgerm
2 tablespoons chopped parsley
1 large, flat mushroom, finely chopped
1 tablespoon cold-pressed olive or sunflower oil
1 egg yolk
1 small bunch spring onions, chopped
1 teaspoon lemon juice
1 heaped teaspoon dried thyme
Pinch marjoram
Dash nutmeg

Salt and pepper

Mix all ingredients and adjust seasoning to taste. Mix with a little water to moisten (it must still be stiff though). Use as a stuffing for chicken or turkey and beef olives.

Special note: This is really delicious and no one would guess that wheatgerm has been used instead of bread crumbs. As bread is a starch, it is not ideal for making stuffings for protein. Wheatgerm is neutral and is suitable for any starch or protein combination.

Vegetable Stuffing

1 onion, finely chopped (I prefer to use chopped celery)
2 teaspoons butter
100 g – 200 g button mushrooms, sliced
½ – 1 cup carrot, grated
1 tablespoon parsley, chopped
1 tablespoon pea flour
1 teaspoon dried mixed herbs
Herbal salt
Pepper
Dash of nutmeg

Sauté onion in the butter. Add all the remaining ingredients except the flour. Cook until the water starts to draw and then add the flour. Cool and use to stuff a whole chicken, or alternatively, lift the skin off chicken pieces and fill with stuffing. Dry roast the chicken in foil for 30 minutes at 200°C and then for a futher hour at 160°C. Serve with neutral vegetables and remember to start with a large salad.

Special note: This stuffing is delicious in baked potatoes.

STARCH DISHES

Starch dishes should be served with a salad or with any neutral vegetable dish. They should never be served with a protein as this is a poor combination.

Chinese Stir-fry

1 cup chopped onion
1 cup chopped celery
1 cup chopped mushrooms
½ cup peas
½ cup sliced green beans
1 cup brown rice
1 tablespoon chopped parsley
MSG-free soy sauce or yeast extract to taste

Stir-fry the vegetables lightly in a little water, adding the mushrooms, parsley and soy sauce last. Add a knob of butter before serving. Start the meal with a large salad.

How to Make Perfect Mashed Potatoes

1 – 2 large potatoes per person
Fresh thin cream or soya milk
Butter
Herbal salt

Steam the potatoes, unpeeled but chopped roughly, in a stainless steel retractable steamer. When done, remove from steamer, pour the water from the pot and mash with a fork or a potato masher. Believe it or not, the skins are quite delicious. The skins also encourage you to chew the potatoes and as you know, chewing gets the starch digesting enzyme working. Add a little butter, thin cream and the salt.

Special note: Mashed potatoes are even more delicious when you fold some lightly steamed mushrooms into the mixture. Mash can also be piped over any vegetable casserole and baked in the oven, like cottage pie.

How to Bake Perfect Potatoes

Choose potatoes of equal size and scrub them thoroughly. Prick the skins with a fork to prevent the potatoes from bursting in the oven. Place on the oven rack and bake at 200°C for 50 – 60 minutes. When ready, remove from the oven and cut a deep cross in the centre of each potato. Press the sides together gently to open the cross. Dot with butter or add a dash of sour cream or cold-pressed olive oil, and sprinkle with chopped parsley. Baked potatoes are perfect for serving with a salad and any neutral vegetable.

Stuffing Baked Potatoes

Bake potatoes in the oven as above. When ready, slice the top off each potato, scoop out the flesh and mash with cold-pressed vegetable oil, butter, cream or soya milk and a little herbal salt. Add steamed, sliced mushrooms and a dash of nutmeg to the mixture, or some chopped steamed spinach. Refill the skins, sprinkle with a little nutmeg and return to a 200°C oven for 10 minutes, or until lightly brown. Serve with a salad and any neutral vegetables.

Oven Chips

Slice as many potatoes as you need into any shape you like. (Most food processors have excellent slicing and chipping blades). Spread the potatoes evenly over a baking sheet and drizzle lightly with oil. Bake in a very hot oven (200° C 220°C) until done. This usually takes about 15 – 25 minutes, depending on how thickly the potatoes are sliced. These chips are delicious when served with an avocado dip (instead of the usual tomato sauce).

Potato Casserole

2 medium potatoes per person
250 ml thin cream or soya milk

Salt and freshly ground black pepper
Spring onion, chopped (optional)
Mushrooms, sliced (optional)

Scrub potatoes thoroughly. Slice into 5 mm slices. Layer potatoes (and onions and mushrooms if using) with seasoning and cream in an oven-proof dish. Bake at 180°C – 200°C for about an hour. Although this dish is very simple, it is quite delicious. Remove the lid of the casserole dish half-way through for a crispy top.

Root Vegetable Casserole

1 cup sweet potatoes
1 cup white potatoes
1 cup parsnips
1 cup carrots
1 cup turnips

Peel vegetables and chop into cubes. Steam until tender and toss in butter, herbal salt, freshly ground pepper and thyme. Serve with a fresh green salad.

Special note: Although pepper is included in many recipes, I seldom use it myself as food tastes so good without it.

Mark's Vegetable Casserole

1 red pepper, sliced or chopped
1 punnet broccoli, cut into bite-size pieces
1 packet baby mealies, cut into bite-size pieces
3 – 4 carrots, cut into strips
1 punnet mushrooms
1 heaped teaspoon yeast extract, dissolved in ½ cup hot water
½ cup sprouted lentils
2 teaspoons curry powder (optional)
1 tin Italian tomatoes (optional)

Combine all ingredients in a casserole dish. Cover with lid and bake at 160° – 180°C for an hour. Mark came up with this recipe on a camping trip and it is delicious served on a bed of brown rice with a fresh green salad.

Special note: Although tinned food is not ideal, it can be used occasionally. Remember to go for only those brands free of artificial additives.

Mushroom Stroganoff

500 g ribbon noodles (eggless)
2 punnets button mushrooms, sliced
2 – 3 sticks celery or 1 onion, chopped
250 ml sour cream
Herbal salt
Freshly ground black pepper

Cook noodles according to the instructions on the packet. Sauté the celery and the mushrooms in a little butter. Season and add the cream. Heat through and serve on top of the noodles.

Special note: On special occasions, sprinkle this dish with Parmesan or pecorino cheese and serve with homemade olive bread (see recipe for Never-Fail Bread). The sauce can also be used with protein dishes or even with rice and potatoes.

Stuffed Cabbage Leaves

1 cabbage
3 – 4 cups cooked rice
1 – 2 cups cooked peas
½ punnet mushrooms, sliced (optional)
Herbal salt
1 teaspoon marjoram
Vegetable stock to cover (Yeast extract in hot water or any MSG-free stock cube)

Blanch the cabbage leaves in boiling water until soft enough to roll up. Mix the rest of the ingredients and divide so that there is enough for all the leaves. Spoon mixture into the centre of each leaf, roll up and place seam-side down in an oven-proof dish. Pour over the vegetable stock and bake covered at 160°C for about 30 minutes. Top with sour cream and chopped chives or spring onions.

Sandy's Rice Salad

3 cups cooked brown rice
1 punnet baby marrows, sliced and steamed
Herbal salt
Black Pepper
1 tablespoon fresh basil, chopped
1 red pepper, chopped
2 – 3 sticks celery, chopped

Mix all the warm ingredients with the seasoning. When cool, add the red pepper and celery. This salad can be served as a meal-in-one with some fresh avocado halves.

Mark's Rice Salad

½ standard salad bowl cooked brown rice
½ tin black olives
2 – 3 avocados, cubed
1 tin haricot beans (optional)
½ cup puréed tomato (optional)
1 red pepper, thinly sliced
1 cup lettuce, shredded
1 – 2 sticks celery, chopped

Combine all ingredients, adding the lettuce and avocado last to avoid a mushy salad.

Special note: Remember that haricot beans are not an ideal food as they are high in both protein and carbohydrates.

This makes them difficult to digest and they are prone to ferment in the stomach causing gas. For this reason it is best to
eat this salad as a meal on its own – it is delicious. I find that
the rice is best if it has not been refrigerated but has been
allowed to cool down to room temperature.

Avocado Noodle Salad

500 g spiral noodles (eggless)
250 ml cream
Herbal salt and freshly ground black pepper
1 punnet black or white mushrooms, sliced (optional)
1 teaspoon origanum
4 tomatoes, diced
4 avocados, diced
Olives (optional extra)

Cook the noodles as directed on the packet. Steam the mushrooms lightly. Drain the noodles and add the cream, seasoning
and mushrooms. Either add the avocado, olives and tomatoes immediately and serve as a hot dish, or allow the noodles to cool before adding the rest of the ingredients and serve
as a salad.

Mushroom Burgers

Wholewheat bread rolls
1 large black mushroom per person
1 – 2 slices tomato per roll
Lettuce

Grill the mushrooms in the oven for about 10 minutes with
a little herbal salt and pepper, or steam them in a steamer.
Butter the rolls and fill with tomato, lettuce and mushroom.
Mashed avocado is a delicious accompaniment and so is a
little yeast extract. Thinly sliced red pepper rings add a nice
tang. For those of you who battle to give up tomato sauce,

make your own by blending tomato purée with herbs, olive oil and seasoning.

Special note: This dish is a wonderful alternative to meat burgers and everyone who has tasted them agrees.

Wholewheat Pizza

(Makes 2 large round pizzas, or 1 very large square.)
1 packet instant dry yeast (10 g)
1 cup wholewheat or brown flour
1 ½ cups white bread flour
4 tablespoons cold-pressed sunflower seed or olive oil
½ teaspoon herbal salt
1 cup warm water

Place all ingredients in a food processor and mix using the plastic dough blade. Mix thoroughly until a ball of very pliable dough is formed. Add extra flour or water if the consistency is not quite right. Roll out into 2 large rounds and place on a baking sheet.

Blend 2 to 3 fresh ripe tomatoes with origanum, salt and freshly ground black pepper in the food processor. Spread this over the pizza bases and bake at the highest oven temperature for 5 or 10 minutes. Remove and add the chopped vegetables of your choice such as red pepper, olives, mushrooms, asparagus, artichokes and baby marrow. Return to the oven for about 10 minutes, cut into slices and serve with a large fresh salad. Add sliced avocado after cooking and you will be amazed at how little you miss the cheese!

Never Fail Wholewheat Bread

12 cups of wholewheat flour
2 packets instant dry yeast (20 g)
3 teaspoons salt
3 teaspoons raw honey
6 – 7 cups of warm water (not hot)

Mix the flour, yeast and salt in a large bowl. Dissolve the honey in a cup of water and add it to the dry ingredients. Keep adding the rest of the water until you have a sticky dough – do not knead. Divide the dough into 2 or 3 balls and place in greased bread tins (2 large or 3 medium tins). Cover with a cloth and allow to rise in a warm place for about 20 minutes. Bake at 200°C for 40 minutes.

Serve with a large salad. Remember to chew slowly so that the starch digesting enzyme in your saliva can act upon the bread.

Special note: Fresh origanum, mixed herbs, destoned olives and grated baby marrow can be added to the dough. Use each on its own or all of them together for a really different treat.

Pasta Dishes

Pasta is so versatile – you can add almost anything to it and it is always tasty. Remember that pasta is a carbohydrate, so in order to combine correctly it must not be eaten with a protein. Always serve pasta with a large, fresh salad.

Mushroom and Red Pepper Noodles

1 punnet mushrooms
1 onion, or a stick of celery (optional)
1 red pepper, chopped
500 g noodles (eggless)
2 teaspoons Marmite dissolved in ½ cup boiling water
Herbal salt
Mixed herbs

Cook noodles according to the instructions on the packet. Lightly stir-fry the onion, red pepper and mushrooms in water. Add the noodles, seasoning and Marmite mixture, heat through and serve.

Spinach Lasagne

1 box flat lasagne sheets (eggless)
½ packet ricotta cheese (about 250 g)
2 bunches spinach
½ bunch celery
5 tomatoes
1 – 2 punnets mushrooms
Herbal salt
Freshly ground black pepper
Dash of nutmeg
2 teaspoons origanum

Prepare the lasagne sheets according to the instructions on the packet. Steam the spinach lightly and chop finely in a food processor. Add the ricotta cheese and sliced mushrooms, and season with salt, pepper and nutmeg. Gently stir-fry the celery and tomatoes. Season with salt and pepper and origanum. Layer in an ovenproof dish – first the spinach mixture, then the noodles and then the tomato mixture. Add a sprinkling of Parmesan cheese and bake at 160°C – 180°C for about 30 minutes.

This dish can be prepared in advance and can either be kept for a day in the fridge before baking, or it can be frozen.

Special note: You will notice that noodles and Ricotta cheese are used in this recipe. Ricotta is very low in protein, as far as animal proteins go, and of all the cheeses it combines best with starch. This dish came about as a result of our love of lasagna. We hated the thought of never eating it again because of the meat and pasta combination. We now find this dish far more appealing than our old favourite. Remember that the seasoning and ingredients can be adjusted to suit your own taste.

Spaghetti and Tomato Sauce

500 g spaghetti noodles (eggless)
1 punnet broccoli, cut into bite-size pieces
1 tin black olives, destoned and chopped
1 – 2 tins tomato purée (additive-free)
* or a few puréed fresh tomatoes*
Mixed herbs

Cook spaghetti according to the instructions on the packet and drain well. For the sauce, steam the broccoli lightly, and combine it with the rest of the ingredients. Heat through. If you like, a carton of cream may be added at this stage but remember that it is high in fat. Season and serve on the spaghetti noodles.

Special note: This dish is a good alternative to Spaghetti Bolognese. Bear in mind that cooked tomatoes are not an ideal food simply because they become acidic during the cooking process.

Fresh Tomato and Olive Pasta

500 g ripe tomatoes
1 bunch spring onions, chopped
½ tin black or green olives, destoned and chopped
½ bottle capers
2 tablespoons chopped parsley
1 teaspoon origanum
2 cloves garlic, crushed (optional)
125 ml cold-pressed sunflower seed or olive oil

Chop the tomatoes and mix with all the other ingredients. This mixture can be heated gently or left to stand overnight and served as a cold sauce over your favourite freshly cooked pasta the next day. The second option is preferable as the sauce is left raw – cooked tomatoes tend to become acidic and should be avoided as far as possible.

Vegetable and Herb Pasta

250 g baby marrows, sliced into julienne strips
250 g broccoli, divided into small sprigs
250 g green beans, sliced
30 ml each of parsley, basil, chives (or spring onions),
*   chopped*
500 g pasta, cooked
Herbal salt

Steam the vegetables lightly. Mix together with the pasta, dot with butter and serve.

Artichoke and Olive Pasta

500 g noodles (eggless)
4 large ripe tomatoes, chopped
1 tin artichokes or asparagus
1 cup black olives in brine, destoned and chopped
¼ cup cold-pressed olive or sunflower seed oil
¼ cup fresh basil, chopped
2 tablespoons chopped parsley

Cook noodles according to the instructions on the packet and drain well. Drain the artichokes and mix with the other ingredients. Serve either hot or cold with a fresh salad.

PROTEIN DISHES

Protein dishes should be served with a fresh salad and any neutral vegetables. They should never accompany starch dishes. I have included very few recipes in this section for a good reason – all animal protein should be cooked as simply as possible, preferably grilled or roasted without added fat. Most people tend to be far too elaborate in their preparation of proteins – remember that simplest is best.

Crunchy Salad

1 medium cabbage, shredded finely
Few sprigs of cauliflower
Celery, chopped
Button mushrooms, sliced
Few almonds (or any other nuts of your preference)

Mix all the ingredients – the quantities are up to you. Blend a fresh tomato with some MSG-free soy sauce for a tasty dressing.

Special note: This salad is a protein meal because of the addition of the nuts which are a concentrated form of protein. If you leave out the nuts, it is a neutral salad.

Grilled Fish

Sole, hake or kingklip fillets
Fresh lemon juice
Salt and pepper

Place the fish on a baking tray. Squeeze some lemon juice over each fillet and season with salt and pepper. Dot with butter and grill on the highest rack of the oven for 5 to 15 minutes, depending on the thickness of the fish. Serve with a fresh salad and any neutral vegetables. An avocado dip is an excellent sauce for grilled fish.

Savoury Baked Fish

Hake or kingklip fillets
1 tomato per person
1 bunch spring onions (enough for 4 people)
Fresh lemon juice
Herbal salt and black pepper

Set the oven at 180°C. Place the fish fillets in an oven-proof dish. Layer the tomato, onion and seasoning over the fish,

159

and squeeze over some lemon juice. Bake for 20 to 30 minutes. Serve with salad and vegetables.

SAUCES AND DRESSINGS

Our favourite salad dressing is an avocado dressing, which is really just one of the dips in the salad section. We add either a little more lemon juice to thin it out, or a little filtred water. You might like to try some of our other favourites – they enhance a wide variety of salads.

Cold-Pressed Sunflower Dressing (Neutral)

½ cup sunflower seed oil (cold-pressed)
½ cup freshly squeezed lemon juice
1 teaspoon herbal salt
Freshly ground black pepper
1 – 2 teaspoons fresh mixed herbs, chopped (origanum,
   thyme and basil are good)

Place all the ingredients in a closed jar or container. Shake well and serve immediately or store in the fridge.

Mayonnaise (Protein)

2 egg yolks
1 teaspoon dry mustard
¼ teaspoon herbal salt
Freshly ground black pepper
30 – 40 ml fresh lemon juice
1 cup cold-pressed olive or sunflower seed oil
   (or a blend of the two)
Dash cayenne pepper (optional)

Place the egg yolks in a food processor with the dry ingredients and blend well using the steel blade. Add the lemon juice slowly, using the pulse button. Add the oil in a very slow stream while the blender is running. A teaspoon of boiling water can be added to thin the mayonnaise if necessary.

Tip: The egg yolks must be at room temperature and the oil must be added very slowly. The processor must be running all the time.

Eggless Mayonnaise (Neutral)

250 ml fresh cream
1 teaspoon honey
½ teaspoon paprika
½ teaspoon dry mustard
½ teaspoon herbal salt
Freshly ground black pepper
1 cup cold-pressed sunflower seed oil
Juice of 1 lemon

Whip the cream until firm. Fold in all the dry ingredients. Continue mixing slowly and add the oil in a thin stream. When the mayonnaise starts to thicken, add the lemon juice.

Hot Sauce (Neutral)

3 – 4 sticks celery
1 punnet mushrooms
250 ml thick cream
1 tin tomato and onion mix (optional)
2 – 4 teaspoons fresh origanum, chopped
Herbal salt
Freshly ground black pepper to taste
Dash nutmeg

Stir-fry the celery and mushrooms in a little water for 5 minutes. Add the tomato and onion mix, herbs and spices, and simmer gently. Lastly, add the cream and heat through. Do not allow to come to the boil after adding the cream. This sauce is good for noodles, rice, potatoes, fish or chicken. Any of the ingredients can be left out or increased for variety.

Some Quick Dressings (Neutral)

- Melted butter and lemon juice is good when poured over any lightly steamed vegetables, grilled chicken or fish. It is particularly delicious over broccoli and baby marrow.
- Freshly-squeezed lemon juice can be drizzled over fresh salads.
- Blended tomato, basil, salt, pepper and a little oil (optional) is a good dressing for salads, vegetables or your favourite pasta.

SOMETHING SWEET

Although sweets and desserts are not ideal from a food combining point of view, the following 'cheats' are suitable for special occasions.

Biscuit Oat Crunchies

2 cups oats
2 cups wholewheat flour
2 cups coconut
1 ½ cups raw honey
1 teaspoon bicarb
250 g butter

Melt the butter and honey in a large pot on the stove. Mix the dry ingredients together and add them to the butter mixture. Press the mixture into a Swiss roll pan and bake for 20 to 25 minutes in a slow oven (140°C – 160°C). Remove from the oven when done, and cut into squares while still hot. Allow to cool in the pan.

Special note: Crunchies are better than most biscuits as they contain a higher level of nutrients and fibre, but they should be regarded as a treat and not an everyday snack.

Wheat-free Crunchies

6 cups oats
2 cups rice flour or millet flour
1 – 1½ cups coconut
½ – 1 cup sesame seeds
2 cups raw honey
500 g butter

Melt the butter and mix with the honey. Add the dry ingredients and mix well. Press the mixture into a Swiss roll pan and bake at 180°C for 15 to 20 minutes.

Special note: Remember that having a cupboard full of 'goodies' is not the sign of a good mother. It is better to show your love for your family by not allowing them to eat badly. Biscuits like these should be an occasional 'treat'.

Date Balls

Place equal quantities of oats, coconut and dates in your food processor fitted with a steel blade and blend until the dates are chopped evenly. Add a bit of filtered water to form a pliable 'dough'. Roll into balls (children love rolling these themselves) and dip in coconut. Place on a plate or eat straight away.

Frozen Fruit Pops

Blend together a variety of fruit mixes and freeze in Tupperware lolly moulds:

– *1 punnet strawberries*
  ¼ cup granadilla pulp
  2 teaspoons orange rind

– *1 pineapple*
  2 mangoes

- *3 mangoes*
  ¼ cup granadilla pulp

- *Overripe bananas*

- *Any fresh fruit juice or blended fruit. Kiwi fruit is especially good.*

Bananas are best peeled and placed whole in a plastic bag and frozen overnight. The next day, blend in a food processor and scoop into a bowl like 'soft serve'. All these frozen fruit pops are delicious and will satisfy any child's craving for ice-cream. They have the additional advantage of being sugar and dairy free, they are loaded with nutrients and are alkaline in the bloodstream.

Pet's Devil Food Cake

5 tablespoons carob powder
300 ml water (or cream and water mixed)
5 egg yolks
100 g butter
1 cup raw honey
1 teaspoon vanilla essence
250 g sifted brown flour
2 teaspoons baking powder
½ teaspoon bicarb

Mix half the water, the carob powder and 1 egg yolk together in a small pot and heat until just below boiling-point. Place the butter, honey and remaining 4 egg yolks in a food processor and blend well. Add the carob mixture and the vanilla essence to the blender. Add the flour, baking powder and bicarb and mix well (use the pulse facility on the blender to avoid over processing). Add the rest of the water, alternating it with the flour. Pour the mixture into 2 standard greased

164

round tins, and bake at 180°C for 25 to 30 minutes. Decorate with the icing of your choice.

Special note: Although cakes are not ideal, there will probably be the odd occasion where you will have to serve one. Egg yolks are used in this recipe as they are not as high in protein as egg whites, and they digest comfortably with starches.

Carrot Cake

1 cup raw honey
250 ml cold pressed oil
3 eggs
375 ml wholewheat flour
10 ml baking powder
10 ml cinnamon
5 ml bicarb
250 ml mashed bananas
250 ml grated carrots
125 ml nuts

Cream honey, oil and eggs. Sift the flour, cinnamon and bicarb together. Add the sugar mixture and the rest of the ingredients to the flour mixture. Mix well. Bake in 2 round cake tins for about 25 minutes at 180°C.

Special note: Although not a wonderful combination, this is a better alternative than 'normal' cake.

Nutritive Value Chart: Nuts and Vegetables

	Grams	Water %	Food Energy Kj	Protein g	Fat g	Saturated g
Nuts (all shelled)						
Almonds (250ml)	130	4,7	3254	24,18	70,46	5,58
Brazil Nuts (250ml)	120	4,6	3286	17,16	80,28	20,50
Cashew Nuts (250ml)	140	5,2	3287	24,08	63,98	10,71
Coconut Desic. (125ml)	40	3,5	1108	2,88	25,96	22,46
Hazelnuts (250ml)	115	5,8	3052	14,49	71,76	5,13
Pecan Nuts (250ml)	120	3,4	3451	11,04	85,44	6,95
Sunflower Seeds (125 ml)	80	4,8	1875	19,2	37,84	4,77
Walnuts (250ml)	120	3,5	3270	11,84	76,8	8,35
Vegetables						
Green Beans, cooked	120	92,4	126	1,92	0,24	0,06
Broccoli, cooked (125ml)	75	91,3	82	2,33	0,23	–
Cabbage, cooked 125ml	80	93,9	67	0,88	0,16	–
Cabbage, raw (250ml)	80	92,4	80	1,04	0,16	–
Carrots (C) (125ml)	80	91,2	104	0,72	0,16	–
Carrots (R) (125ml)	80	88,2	141	0,88	0,16	–
Cauliflower (C) (125ml)	80	92,8	74	1,84	0,16	–
Cauliflower (R) (125ml)	80	91	90	2,16	0,16	–
Cucumber (5 slices)	50	95,7	30	0,3	0,05	–
Green Peas (C)	85	81,5	252	4,59	0,34	0,16
Lettuce	100	95,9	53	1,0	0,2	0,03
Potato (Boiled)	90	82,8	245	1,71	0,09	0,02
Summer Gem Squash (C)	75	95,5	44	0,68	0,08	–
Winter Hubbard Squash (C)	125	88,8	199	1,38	0,38	–
Spinach (C)	90	92	86	2,70	0,27	0,04
Sweet Potato (C)	145	72	526	1,60	0,87	0,42
Tomato	200	93,5	184	2,2	0,4	–

R = raw   C = cooked   – No reliable data

Nutritive Value Chart: Nuts and Vegetables

	Grams g	Monounsat g	Polyunsat g	Carbohydrate g	Calcium mg	Iron mg	Vitamin A iu
Nuts (all shelled)							
Almonds (250ml)	130	48,22	13,21	6,8	304	6,11	0
Brazil Nuts (250ml)	120	26,33	29,93	5,16	223	4,08	0
Cashew Nuts (250ml)	140	42,83	4,02	39,1	53	5,32	140
Coconut Desic. (125ml)	40	1,50	0,47	2,5	10	1,32	0
Hazelnuts (250ml)	115	55,6	7,48	7,9	240	3,91	0
Pecan Nuts (250ml)	120	49,33	20,42	17,5	88	2,88	156
Sunflower Seeds (125 ml)	80	7,0	24,26	12,7	96	5,68	40
Walnuts (250ml)	120	11,96	52,42	11,0	119	3,72	36
Vegetables							
Green Beans, cooked	120	0,01	0,17	3,1	60	0,72	648
Broccoli, cooked (125ml)	75	–	–	0,8	66	0,6	1,875
Cabbage, cooked (125ml)	80	–	–	1,2	35	0,24	104
Cabbage, raw (250ml)	80	–	–	2,6	39	0,32	104
Carrots (C) (125ml)	80	–	–	3,2	26	0,48	8,400
Carrots (R) (125ml)	80	–	–	5,0	30	0,56	8,800
Cauliflower (C) (125ml)	80	–	–	1,4	17	0,56	48
Cauliflower (R) (125ml)	80	–	–	2,1	20	0,88	48
Cucumber (5 slices)	50	–	–	1,4	9	0,15	0
Green Peas (C)	85	0,14	0,04	6,0	20	1,53	459
Lettuce	100	0,01	0,10	0,6	19	0,5	330
Potato (Boiled)	90	0,01	0,06	2,0	5	0,45	0
Summer Gem Squash (C)	75	–	–	12,2	19	0,3	293
Winter Hubbard Squash (C)	125	–	–	10,1	25	0,63	4,375
Spinach (C)	90	0,03	0,21	0,2	84	1,98	7,290
Sweet Potato (C)	145	0,07	0,36	29,1	30	0,87	9,667
Tomato	200	–	–	6,4	26	1,0	1,800

R = raw   C = cooked   – No reliable data

Nutritive Value Chart: Nuts and Vegetables

	Grams	Thiamin mg	Riboflavin mg	Nicotinic Acid mg	Vitamin B6 mg	Folic Acid mg	Ascorbic Acid (Vit C) mg
Nuts (all shelled)							
Almonds (250ml)	130	0,31	1,20	4,55	0,13	125	tr
Brazil Nuts (250ml)	120	1,15	0,14	1,92	0,212	5	tr
Cashew Nuts (250ml)	140	0,60	0,35	2,52	–	95	0
Coconut Desic. (125ml)	40	0,02	0,02	0,24	0,018	10	0
Hazelnuts (250ml)	115	0,53	–	1,04	1,012	132	tr
Pecan Nuts (250ml)	120	1,03	0,16	1,08	0,22	29	2
Sunflower Seeds (125 ml)	80	1,56	0,18	4,32	1,0	186	0
Walnuts (250ml)	120	0,40	0,16	1,08	1,104	100	2
Vegetables							
Green Beans, cooked	120	0,08	0,11	0,6	0,068	59	14
Broccoli, cooked (125ml)	75	0,07	0,15	0,6	0,084	71	68
Cabbage, cooked (125ml)	80	0,03	0,03	0,24	0,08	28	26
Cabbage, raw (250ml)	80	0,04	0,04	0,24	0,08	46	38
Carrots (C) (125ml)	80	0,04	0,04	0,40	0,072	6	5
Carrots (R) (125ml)	80	0,05	0,04	0,48	0,14	14	6
Cauliflower (C) (125ml)	80	0,07	0,06	0,48	0,126	51	44
Cauliflower (R) (125ml)	80	0,09	0,08	0,56	0,197	38	62
Cucumber (5 slices)	50	0,02	0,02	0,1	0,024	10	6
Green Peas (C)	85	0,24	0,09	1,96	0,078	45	17
Lettuce	100	0,05	0,03	0,2	0,04	56	4
Potato (Boiled)	90	0,07	0,03	0,99	0,131	9	13
Summer Gem Squash (C)	75	0,04	0,06	0,6	0,038	8	8
Winter Hubbard Squash (C)	125	0,05	0,13	0,50	0,159	34	10
Spinach (C)	90	0,06	0,13	0,45	0,087	68	25
Sweet Potato (C)	145	0,12	0,06	0,87	0,189	36	22
Tomato	200	0,12	0,08	1,4	0,220	56	46

R = raw   C = cooked   tr = Trace or small amount   – No reliable data

168

Nutritive Value Chart: Fruit

	Apples	Apricots	Avocados	Bananas	Cherries	Dates	Figs Dried	Goose-berries	Grana-dillas
Grams (g)	160	50	125	80	68	50	20	75	60
Water (%)	83,9	86,4	74,3	74,3	80,8	22,5	28,4	87,9	72,9
Food Energy (Kj)	392	101	843	307	204	576	214	140	245
Protein (g)	0,32	0,70	2,5	0,8	0,82	1,0	0,62	0,68	1,32
Fat (g)	0,64	0,2	19,13	0,40	0,68	0,25	0,24	0,45	0,42
Saturated (g)	0,10	0,02	3,05	0,15	0,15	–	0,05	0,03	–
Monounsat (g)	0,03	0,09	12,01	0,03	0,18	–	0,05	0,04	–
Polyunsat (g)	0,18	0,04	2,45	0,07	0,20	–	0,11	0,24	–
Carbohydrate (g)	19,5	4,5	6,6	16,3	10,3	32,8	9,9	5,7	4,5
Calcium (mg)	11,0	7,0	14,0	5,0	10,0	16,0	29,0	19,0	7,0
Iron (mg)	0,32	0,25	1,25	0,24	0,27	0,6	0,44	0,23	0,96
Vitamin A (iu)	85,0	1306	765,0	65,0	146,0	25,0	27,0	218,0	420,0
Thiamin (mg)	0,03	0,02	0,14	0,04	0,03	0,05	0,01	0,03	tr
Riboflavin (mg)	0,02	0,02	0,15	0,08	0,04	0,05	0,01	0,02	0,08
Nicotinic Acid (mg)	0,16	0,03	2,38	0,4	0,27	1,1	0,14	0,23	0,9
Vitamin B6 (mg)	0,077	0,027	0,35	0,462	0,024	0,096	0,045	0,06	–
Folic Acid (mg)	5,0	5,0	78,0	15,0	3,0	7,0	2,0	–	–
Ascorbic Acid (mg) (Vit C)	10,0	5,0	10,0	7,0	5,0	–	tr	21,0	18,0

Nutritive Value Chart: Fruit

	Grape-fruit	Grapes	Guavas	Kiwi Fruit	Lemons	Loquats	Litchi	Mangoes	Melons Yellow
Grams (g)	120	250	75	100	75	60	80	350	250
Water (%)	90,9	80,6	86,1	80,5	89,0	86,7	81,8	81,7	89,8
Food Energy (Kj)	161	743	158	281	92	118	221	956	370
Protein (g)	0,72	1,75	0,60	1,0	0,83	0,24	0,64	1,75	2,25
Fat (g)	0,12	1,5	0,45	0,6	0,23	0,12	0,32	1,05	0,75
Saturated (g)	0,01	0,48	0,13	–	0,03	0,02	–	0,25	–
Monounsat (g)	0,01	0,05	0,05	–	0,01	0,01	–	0,35	–
Polyunsat (g)	0,02	0,43	0,19	–	0,08	0,05	–	0,18	–
Carbohydrate (g)	9,0	40,3	4,7	14,2	6,8	7,0	12,8	53,9	17,0
Calcium (mg)	14,0	28,0	15,0	29,0	20,0	10,0	4,0	35,0	28,0
Iron (mg)	0,12	0,75	0,23	0,4	0,45	0,18	0,24	0,35	0,5
Vitamin A (iu)	149,0	183,0	593,0	–	22,0	917,0	0	13629,0	8060,0
Thiamin (mg)	0,05	0,23	0,04	0,02	0,03	0,01	0,01	0,21	0,1
Riboflavin (mg)	0,02	0,15	0,04	0,01	0,02	0,01	0,06	0,21	0,05
Nicotinic Acid (mg)	0,36	0,75	0,9	0,2	0,08	0,12	0,48	2,1	1,5
Vitamin B6 (mg)	0,05	0,275	0,107	–	0,06	–	–	0,469	0,288
Folic Acid (mg)	12,0	10,0	–	–	8,0	–	–	–	43,0
Ascorbic Acid (mg) (Vit C)	41,0	28,0	138,0	118,0	40,0	1,0	58,0	98,0	108,0

Nutritive Value Chart: Fruit

	Melons Green	Naartjies	Oranges	Pawpaw	Peaches	Pears	Pineapples	Plums	Prickly Pears
Grams (g)	250	105	130	80	150	220	85	50	75
Water (%)	89,7	87,6	86,8	88,8	87,7	83,8	86,5	85,2	87,6
Food Energy (Kj)	370	193	256	129	270	543	176	115	129
Protein (g)	1,25	0,63	1,17	0,48	1,05	0,88	0,34	0,4	0,53
Fat (g)	0,25	0,21	0,13	0,08	0,15	0,88	0,34	0,30	0,45
Saturated (g)	–	0,02	0,03	0,03	0,02	0,04	0,03	0,03	–
Monounsat (g)	–	0,03	0,03	0,03	0,05	0,18	0,04	0,21	–
Polyunsat (g)	–	0,04	0,04	0,02	0,08	0,20	0,13	0,07	–
Carbohydrate (g)	19,0	9,8	12,7	7,1	14,9	27,7	9,3	5,5	5,9
Calcium (mg)	15,0	15,0	52,0	19,0	8,0	24,0	6,0	2,0	42,0
Iron (mg)	0,25	0,11	0,13	0,08	0,15	0,66	0,34	0,05	0,23
Vitamin A (iu)	100,0	966,0	267,0	1611	803,0	44,0	20,0	161,0	38,0
Thiamin (mg)	0,2	0,12	0,12	0,02	0,03	0,04	0,08	0,02	0,01
Riboflavin (mg)	0,05	0,02	0,05	0,02	0,06	0,09	0,03	0,05	0,05
Nicotinic Acid (mg)	1,5	0,21	0,39	0,24	1,5	0,22	0,34	0,25	0,38
Vitamin B6 (mg)	0,148	0,07	0,078	0,015	0,027	0,04	0,074	0,041	–
Folic Acid (mg)	133,0	21,0	39,0	–	5,0	15,0	9,0	1,0	–
AscorbicAcid (mg) (Vit C)	63,0	33,0	69,0	50,0	11,0	9,0	13,0	5,0	11,0

Nutritive Value Chart: Fruit

	Prunes Dried	Raisins	Straw-berries	Water melon
Grams (g)	80	80	85	100
Water (%)	32,4	15,4	91,6	91,5
Food Energy (Kj)	800	1002	108	132
Protein (g)	2,08	2,56	0,51	0,6
Fat (g)	0,04	0,40	0,34	0,4
Saturated (g)	0,03	0,12	0,02	–
Monounsat (g)	0,27	0,02	0,04	–
Polyunsat (g)	0,09	0,11	0,16	–
Carbohydrate (g)	38,8	57,4	4,3	6,9
Calcium (mg)	41,0	39,0	12,0	8,0
Iron (mg)	2,0	1,68	0,34	0,2
Vitamin A (iu)	1590	6,0	23,0	366,0
Thiamin (mg)	0,06	0,13	0,02	0,08
Riboflavin (mg)	0,13	0,07	0,06	0,02
Nicotinic Acid (mg)	116,0	0,64	0,17	0,2
Vitamin B6 (mg)	0,208	0,199	0,05	0,144
Folic Acid (mg)	3,0	2,0	15,0	2,0
Ascorbic Acid (mg) (Vit C)	2,0	2,0	48,0	10,0

These nutritive value charts are adapted from the National Research Institute for Nutritional Diseases (NRIND) of the South African Medical Research Council (SAMRC).

– No reliable data
tr Trace or small amount

NATURAL WAY EATING CHART

- Eat fruit by itself on an empty stomach for at least one meal per day. Fruit can replace any meal

ACID FRUIT	→ GOOD COMBINATION →	SUB-ACID FRUIT	→ GOOD COMBINATION →	SWEET FRUIT
Goes well with sub-acid fruits		Goes well with acid and sweet fruits		Goes well with sub-acid fruits
Gooseberries		Apple		Banana
Granadilla		Apricot		Dates
Grapefruit		Berries		Fig
Guava		Cherries		Papino
Kiwi fruit		Grapes		Pawpaw
Kumquats		Litchis		Persimmon
Lemon		Loquats		Prunes
Lime		Mango		Raisins
Melons		Nectarine		Sultanas (Unbleached)
Naartjie		Peach		
Orange		Pear		
Pineapple		Prickly pear		
Pomegranate				
Quince				
Spanspek				
Strawberries				
Tangerine				
Watermelon				

- Wait 40-60 minutes after eating fruit before eating other foods
- Nuts can be eaten with any acid fruit
- Fruit can be eaten 3 – 4 hours after any other meal
- All melons (including spanspek and watermelon) are best eaten alone
- The daily menu should consist of 75% raw fruits and vegetables

173

NATURAL WAY EATING CHART

- Eat **one** protein at a time (preferably once a day only) as a main course with a large salad and/or neutral vegetables
- Eat **one** starch at a time as a main course with a large salad and/or neutral vegetables
- Fats (butter*, cream*, cold-pressed oils), taken in small quantities combine with neutral vegetables, starch or proteins

*PROTEINS — GOOD COMBINATION	*NEUTRAL VEGETABLES — GOOD COMBINATION	*STARCH
Combine well with neutral vegetables	Combine well with protein or starch	Combine well with neutral vegetables
Eggs°	Artichoke, Asparagus,	Barley
Dairy products°	Aubergine (brinjal), Avocado,	Bread
Fish°	Beetroot, Broccoli,	Buckwheat
Meat+	Brussels sprouts, Butternut,	Cereals
Milk+	Cabbage, Carrot, Cauliflower,	Jerusalem artichoke
Nuts (also coconut)	Celery, Courgette (baby marrow),	Maize (mealies/corn)
Poultry°	Cucumber, Fennel, Garlic,	Millet
Seeds (sunflower,	Gem squash, Green beans,	Oats
sesame, etc.)	Herbs, Leeks, Lettuce, Marrow,	Pasta
Unprocessed cheese°	Mushrooms, Okra, Olives, Onions,	Potatoes
Yoghurt°	Parsley, Peas (fresh),	Rice
	Peppers (green, red, yellow),	Rice cakes
	Pumpkin, Radishes, Shallots,	Rye
	Spinach, Spring onions, Sprouts,	Sweet Potatoes
	Squashes, Tomato, Turnip,	Wheat
	Waterblommetjie, Watercress	

+ *Should be minimised*
° *Once or twice a week in small quantities*

* **Wait at least 3 hours after eating these foods before eating fruit again**
  - Protein-starch combinations are difficult to digest and are prone to fermentation
- All legumes (such as beans, lentils and peanuts) are high in starch and protein and result in digestive discomfort
- The Natural Way programme has been designed for complete and efficient digestion, weight-loss, high energy and glowing health

If you have any questions about changing to the Natural Way life-style, write to me at the following address:

Mary-Ann Shearer
P O Box 784211
Sandton 2146
Republic of South Africa

Kindly enclose a self addressed, stamped envelope. Please bear in mind that as I answer all my mail personally, a reply might take a few weeks.

If you would like details of our 'Mail Order' service, please write to me at the above address.

Other titles by the author:
The Natural Way Recipe Book I
The Natural Way Recipe Book II

Look out for the forthcoming *Natural Way Library*, a series of booklets covering a variety of health-related topics in greater detail and answering some common vexing questions.

References and Further Reading

Beukes, V. *Killer Foods of the Twentieth Century*. Johannesburg: Perskor, 1974.

Bieler, Dr H M. *Food is your Best Medicine*. Great Britain: Neville Spearman, 1968.

Budd, Martin L. *Low Blood Sugar*. Great Britain: Thorsons, 1984.

Cheraskin, Dr E. *Diet and Disease*. Connecticut: Keats, 1968.

College of Natural Hygiene. *The Life Science Health System*. Manchaca, Texas.

Diet, Life-style and Mortality in China: A Study of the Characteristics of 65 Chinese Countries. Cornel University Press and People's Medical Publishing House, 1990.

Dufty, William. *Sugar Blues*. Warner Books.

Ehret, Prof Arnold. *Mucousless Diet Healing System*. Ehret Lit. Publishing.

Ganong, William F. *Review of Medical Physiology*.

Garrison, Robert H and Somer, Elizabeth. *The Nutrition Desk Reference*. USA, 1990.

Gilbert, Zoë and Hadfield, Jack. *Down to Earth Fruit and Vegetable Gardening in South Africa*. Cape Town: CNA, 1987.

Grant, Doris and Joice, Jean. *Food Combining for Health*. Great Britain: Thorsons, 1984.

Green, J H. *Basic Clinical Physiology*. Great Britain: Oxford Medical Press.

Guyton's Medical Physiology. (Seventh edition) USA.

Haas, Dr Robert. *Eat to Win*. USA Penguin Books, 1983.

Hansen, Maurice. *E for Additives*. Great Britain: Thorsons.

Hay, Dr W H. *A New Health Era*. London: Harrap & Co, 1934.

Honiball, Essie. *I Live on Fruit*. Pretoria: Makro Books, 1981.

Kenton, Lesley. *Raw Energy*. London: Arrow Books, 1984.

Kenton, Lesley. *The Biogenic Diet*. London: Arrow Books, 1986.

Mendelsohn, Robert S. *Confessions of a Medical Heretic*. USA: Warner.

Meyer, Prof B J. *Fruit for Thought*. Pretoria: Haum, 1979.

Milstone, Eric and Abraham, John. *Additives: A Guide for Everyone*. London: Penguin Books, 1988.

Nelson, Dennis. *Food Combining Simplified*. 1983.

Pavlov, Prof Ivan. *The Work of the Digestive System*. Clark & Griffin.

Pfeiffer, Dr Carl. *Total Nutrition*. Great Britain: Granada, 1982.

Pottenger, Dr T M. *Pottenger's Cats*. Pottenger Foundation.

Price, Weston, A. *Nutrition and Physical Degeneration*. USA: Keats, 1945.

Rahway, N J. *The Merck Manual* (Fifteenth edition). Merck, Sharp and Dohme Research Labs, 1987.

Schauss, A G. *Nutrition and Behaviour*. USA: Keats, 1988.

Scott, Caryl Vaughan. *Whole Energy*. Johannesburg: Pouyoukas, 1985.

Tobe, John H. *Margarine*. Canada: Provoker Press, 1962.

Webb, Tony and Lang, Dr Tim. *Irradiation: The Facts*. London: Thorsons, 1987.

Wilson, Frank Avray. *Food Fit For Humans*. London: C W Daniel & Co, 1975.

World Book Medical Encyclopaedia.

Index

178

183

University, Chinese research, 12-13, 48-9, 54, 62

P
Pakistan people, role of diet in health, 13
Pasta dishes, 155-8
Peanuts, 24, 56
Pepsin, 26
Pet's Devil Food Cake, 126, 164-5
Phosphorus, 27, 81
Phytic acid, 19
Piccioni, Richard, 69
Pickles, compostion, 66
Polasch, P, 87, 88-9
Polony, composition, 66
Polyunsaturated fats, 61-2
Poor eating habits, 10, 12, 13, 81
Posture, 77
Potato Casserole, 149-50
Potatoes, 25, 31
  baked, 149
  mashed, 148
Pottenger, F M, 44-5, 69
Pottenger's Cats, 44, 69
Pre-menstrual tension, 38
Preparation of food, 128-30
Preservatives, 55, 60, 64, 65-7, 120, 121, 129
  in skin care products, 83
Processed foods, composition, 55, 66, 68
Protein, 17, 24
  and alcohol, 113
  combining, 6, 21, 24, 174
  composition, 25-6, 52
  consequences of high protein

diet, 41-2, 53, 54, 56
content in fruit, 53-4
daily requirement, 31, 53, 56
digestion of, 26, 49
and exercise, 75
Protein dishes, 131-2, 158-60
  Crunchy Salad, 159
  Grilled Fish, 159
  Savoury Baked Fish, 159-60
  Protein *see also* Animal products, Cheese, Chicken, Eggs, Fish, Meat
Ptyalin, 16, 25, 26, 138

R
Radurization *see* Irradiation
Ratatouille, quick and simple, 142
Rebounding, 72-3, 118
Recipes, 131-64
Refined foods, consumption and its effects, 13, 41-4, 75
Reproduction and diet, 57-8
Rest during fasting, 92-3
Rice Salad, 151
Root Vegetable Casserole, 150
Roti, 146
Runny noses, 4, 5, 6, 27, 46

S
Saccharin, 68
St Martin, Alexis, 23
Salad dressings, composition, 66
Salads, 28, 51, 133-8
Salisbury, James, 26-7
Sandy's Cauliflower Salad, 138
Sandy's Rice Salad, 151
Saturated fats, 19, 61, 62
Sauces, composition, 65, 66, 68

yes